Elite Financial Teams

Elite Financial Teams

The 17% Solution

Matt Oechsli

Wealth Management Press
9800 Metcalf Ave.
Overland Park, KS 66212

First edition.

Designed and typeset by Sans Serif Inc., Saline, MI
Cover design by KCL Creative, Ramseur, NC
Printed in the United States of America

ISBN: 0-9656765-6-0

Contents

Introduction

Teamwork.

It's an ideal to which most of us aspire, but which few actually achieve.

In the business community, managers constantly strive to build better teams—to assemble the skills, talents and visions of various individuals into synchronized profit-making machines. The *ideal* of teamwork is so finely woven into the fabric of American society that many people automatically condemn anyone who dares question the need for teams or impugns their effectiveness. *That* is un-American. *That* is like telling a classroom of kindergarteners that Santa Claus is a besotted old fake.

Well, I'm not about to pull the beard off Kris Kringle at Macy's this Christmas, but I *will* "de-beard" the notion that calling a loose confederation of financial service professionals a "financial team" causes them *to work together as a team.*

This book is designed, in part, to help you distinguish Elite Financial Teams from the masses, many of whom are disorganized, dysfunctional confederations of financial professionals. The former will almost always succeed while the latter will always be challenged, and many will fail. Unfortunately, many financial services professionals cobble together for the wrong reasons, hoping the blessings of "teamwork" will be conferred upon them and bestow miracles.

That is a very dangerous illusion.

There are no miracles.

It takes hard "work" to build an effective "team."

If I were a cynic, I'd argue that most financial teams are created as marketing ploys. I would argue that the financial services industry is blindly following the example set by Goldman Sachs years ago—without a clue as to why that system was developed and why it works for Goldman.

I won't argue those points, but based on four years of research conducted by The Oechsli Institute, it's evident *why* most teams are *not* successful and why they *won't* become successful any time soon.

The good news is: there are distinct reasons why some teams succeed and others don't. Once you identify these reasons and take the steps suggested herein, you will dramatically increase your chances of launching a powerhouse team.

The 17% Solution

Most of what we read about financial teams focuses on the success stories—the top performers, the paragons of leadership, business savvy, financial acumen and salesmanship. But according to our criteria, only 17% of financial teams fall into this category. That 17% attracts more new affluent clients every year (per senior partner) with at least $1,000,000 in investable assets than their counterparts, solo or team. In addition, the elite teams succeed at retaining and *upgrading* their existing affluent clients by delivering the full array of wealth management services the affluent want.

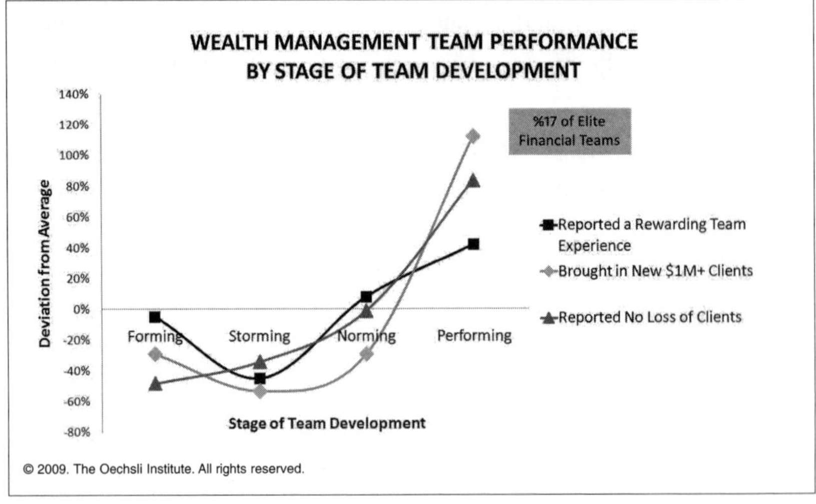

What we *don't* hear are the secrets *behind* their success, and why the other 83% of teams struggle—some at high production levels; others just to achieve mediocre results.

Therefore, to determine what (if any) secrets these top teams possessed, The Oechsli Institute commissioned two studies on how financial teams developed. Our objective was to discover *what separates the best from all the rest.* We sampled more than 1,350 financial team members in a variety of organizational settings—from wirehouses and regional firms to independents and RIAs, as well as the CPAs and insurance professionals associated with financial teams.

This book is based, in part, on the materials drawn from three research reports:

- 2003 Developing an Elite Financial Team
- 2007 Creating an Elite Financial Team
- 2009 Leading an Elite Financial Team in Tough Times

The Oechsli Institute, Jacokes & Associates and Dr. John Eatman worked together to research numerous aspects of the financial services industry related to attracting, servicing and retaining affluent investors. Our emphasis was on defining the needs, perceptions, realities and performance gaps waiting to be addressed. We also wanted to discover how financial teams progressed through the stages of team development. For this purpose, we used the widely accepted *Forming, Storming, Norming* and *Performing* team development model created by Dr. Bruce Tuckman of Ohio State University. Ultimately, we wanted to identify the specific criteria that separate Elite Financial Teams from the rest, so we could create a working model of an elite 21st Century financial team.

The results of the study were fascinating, enabling us to determine the following:

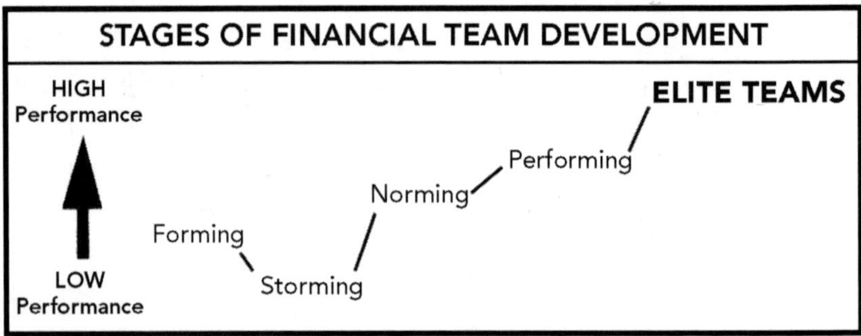

To achieve elite status, financial teams must work their way through Dr. Tuckman's 4 stages of team development. In sum, these are:

—*The Forming Stage.* Individual roles and responsibilities are unclear, and team members are often guarded in their interactions. Members are totally dependent on the Team Leader for guidance and direction.

—*The Storming Stage.* As members frequently challenge each other, strained relations emerge. The leader strives to resolve conflicts and focus efforts toward the next stage.

—*The Norming Stage.* Individual roles and responsibilities become clear and accepted. Team members work hard to reach consensus. Commitment and unity are strong, and members are not as dependent on the leader as they once were. Although the team experiences cohesion, elite status still eludes them.

—*The Performing Stage.* The team clearly knows the direction they are taking and why. Members work together to achieve goals, strengthen relationships and support each other's efforts. People work well individually, in small groups and as a team. Essentially, the leader delegates, coordinates and participates with the team.

The principles highlighted in this book are designed to propel teams through the four stages of development on their way to elite status. To be sure, the rewards for performing at a high level are plentiful, but the cost of entry is steep. Here are some of our findings:

- Financial teams do not achieve elite status quickly or by accident. It requires both desire and a focused effort to achieve elite status.
- There are 15 Performance Factors that can be used as benchmarks. These benchmarks enabled us to create a 5-part team model: Team Leadership, Business Development Process, Client Loyalty Process, Wealth Management Process and Practice Management Process.
- Financial teams can evolve through the predictable stages of team development by working to improve each of the 15 Performance Factors in the Elite Financial Team model.
- As financial teams take action to improve performance, they achieve significantly higher results and the team experience becomes more rewarding.
- Elite Financial Teams embrace the Japanese concept of Kaizen: ongoing improvement. They are always striving to get better.

Opportunities and Challenges

We have identified both opportunities and challenges for today's financial teams. The biggest challenges are: (1) most financial teams are, in some capacity, work groups of convenience, and (2) approximately half of financial advisors are sole practitioners who lack the support necessary to provide comprehensive wealth management services—the kind that will overcome the deep-rooted skepticism of affluent investors.

That said, any well-run financial team can capture affluent clients from anyone other than another well-run financial team. Period!

Let's do the math.

Assuming that 50% of all advisors are on a financial team, and with research telling us that just 17% of teams perform at high levels, that leaves 8.5% of all financial professionals qualified to work with the affluent. In other words, there is very little competition! In today's current financial environment, this is becoming increasingly evident.

Naturally, there is no simple answer to the disparity between the successful and the masses of other financial teams, just as there are no easy answers when it comes to raising a functional family. But there are basic precepts than can promote and preserve the health of a family or team (and teams are very much like families).

The main precept is that teams must be formed for the right reasons, and the participants must possess both common goals and common values. Too many groups form for the wrong reasons; too many groups form because it's fashionable; too many groups form because members have hidden agendas. This guarantees that storm clouds will gather, and divorce will be inevitable. And divorce is never easy on either the parents or the "children"—in this case, the clients.

In these "divorces," however, the "children" are less likely to suffer more than the parents, because savvy and skeptical affluent clients usually move to a new "family" long before the dysfunctional family (team) tears itself apart.

The remainder of this book is designed to help you on two fronts (in no order of priority):

1. Improve your ability to attract, service, and develop loyal affluent clients.
2. Enable you to use our team model to benchmark your team against the 15 Performance Factors our research consistently found in-play within Elite Financial Teams.

—Matt Oechsli

SECTION I

Overview of Teams and the Affluent

1

The Affluent Need a Team

The affluent are looking for a solutions provider for the multi-dimensional aspects of their family's financial affairs.
—Factoid, Understanding the Affluent Research

For more than 10 years, The Oechsli Institute has studied the world of the affluent (the top quintile of U.S. income earners), conducting many research projects in an effort to better understand them. Most recently, we commissioned an independent study ("Understanding the Affluent: America's Top Quintile Income Earners") to identify affluent consumers' key motivators. Thanks to this research, we've learned a great deal about what makes the affluent tick. This illustrates the synergy between understanding the affluent (well enough to consistently meet their needs and expectations) and Elite Financial Teams (understanding how these teams have mastered both the challenges of working as teams and working with the affluent).

What the Affluent Want

According to The Oechsli Institute's study, "Understanding the Affluent: America's Top Quintile Income Earners," affluent investors want and NEED your advice and counsel. They are desperately searching for trusted financial professionals or teams of professionals to coordinate *every aspect* of their families' financial affairs. They need someone who is unbiased, knowledgeable and always considers their best interests when making decisions. But most do NOT know where to find these individuals or *teams of individuals.*

Affluent investors who already have financial professionals display significant dissatisfaction with every facet of their relationships. As our research revealed, this offers a *major* opportunity for financial teams to demonstrate that *they* understand the reasons for the dissatisfaction and will correct the problems!

If you want to significantly increase your odds of becoming *the* "go-to" financial team for affluent investors, here are 8 criteria to consider. They were culled from our "Understanding the Affluent" study, with each being statistically significant and the numbering below bears no relevance on the degree of importance assigned by our survey's high-net-worth respondents:

1. Show a clear understanding of the client's goals and family situation.
2. Clearly reveal your fee structure.
3. Proactively contact clients when anything might impact their portfolio.
4. Help select the best asset mix for the client's portfolio.
5. Avoid using technical jargon.
6. Coordinate all of the client's investment decisions.
7. Create and execute a formal financial plan.
8. Help to coordinate and organize all of the client's financial documents.

Now, let's combine the above data with data gathered from another Oechsli Institute study entitled, "How the Affluent Make Purchasing Decisions" (yes we commission a lot of studies). This revealed 7 qualities associated with how the affluent make major purchase decisions, which were (again) ranked in terms of importance. Although these stats apply to *any* major purchase decision—from flat-screen TV's and luxury cars to general contractors and financial planners—they are particularly applicable to financial professionals:

1. Two criteria stood above the rest: 83.3% said that offering the right set of features was very important; 75.8% said that being able to find the best possible option through careful evaluation and comparison was very important.
2. 65.5% said that the opinions of immediate family members and trusted friends had a very significant impact on deciding where to look for options when making a major purchase decision, but only 37.8% said those opinions had a very significant impact on the *final* purchase decision.
3. Once the search process is underway, the affluent place more confidence in their own ability to find information, sort through options, and make the final decision. Respondents also indicated that the Internet and trusted periodicals serve as major research vehicles.
4. When given an opportunity to write in other criteria important to making major purchase decisions, warranties and guarantees won by a wide margin.
5. Even though respondents were extremely price/value conscious, finding a discounted or sale price was not as critical to their final decision.
6. Problem resolution and post-purchase service rated as having the greatest impact on repeat business. Offering the lowest price ranked last.
7. Respondents gave far less importance to reviews and testimonials than they did to the responsiveness of sales and service people.

Please make a *major* mental note of the second quality: the affluent rely on family members and trusted friends when making major purchase decisions. What this means is that financial teams must be "the real deal" before they can hope to win referrals from coveted clients—the affluent individuals and families who put the "wealth" into "wealth management."

Four Key Affluent Motivators

Because aging baby-boomers are the wealthiest generation in history—but NEVER call them "aging" to their faces—with so much money in (or about to be in) transition, understanding their psychographic profile is a must.

Psychographics describes a specific market segment on the basis of psychological characteristics relating to values, attitudes, interests or lifestyles. When an assessment of a specific population is created, the findings are referred to as a psychographic profile. Once introduced to these motivators, you won't be able to read a newspaper, watch the news, or listen to a politician without thinking of them. From our research, we divided the baby boomer profile into *Four Key Affluent Motivators for Life's Decision Making:*

Personal Health

"I need to get in shape."
"I hope my insurance will cover this procedure."
"My blood pressure is sky high."
"I've got to get away from all this stress."
"If only I had time to exercise."

Can you identify with any of these statements?

I can, and odds are that so can nearly all of the affluent in your market. Ten years ago, most of your affluent clients had no clue about their cholesterol level. Today, many are on special diets or take medication to keep it under control.

I'm not suggesting that you start selling long-term care (though it's not a bad idea). I just want to emphasize the importance that personal health plays in your affluent clients' decision-making. Your challenge is to be aware of the financial implications, such as providing both the planning and protection required to meet their needs. You should be aware of current or potential health issues, and address this motivator properly.

Family Health

"My kids will soon be out of the house."

"Maybe we should splurge on that big family vacation."

"I'd like to buy that second home."

"I hope my mother's long-term care doesn't wipe us out."

"Maybe we should downsize."

"I wonder if my mother-in-law will need a nursing home."

As the affluent mature and their children get older, priorities shift.

Although the affluent send their children to college, they consider higher education a hygiene factor. *They expect it.* This is why you must make sure that their college funding is in order. Just don't invest too much emotional energy here, because your affluent clients won't. Many of these family motivators revolve around serious financial issues, which typically boil down to lifestyle. So, think in terms of becoming your affluent client's lifestyle guardian.

Financial Health

"Cash flow is tight, but I need to maintain our lifestyle."

"I wonder if I'm getting the unbiased financial advice I need."

"There's got to be some way to get more deductions."

"I hope we can maintain our lifestyle when I retire."

"I need to get someone to review my financial plan."

"I hate this financial paperwork. I don't even know where our important papers are."

Keep in mind that your affluent clients do not consider themselves wealthy. They don't like to be referred to as affluent or high net worth. Why? Because they've been "worker bees" their entire lives. The graph below speaks volumes:

Today's affluent *are* concerned about their financial affairs, and don't trust the government, Social Security, Medicare *or* the financial services industry.

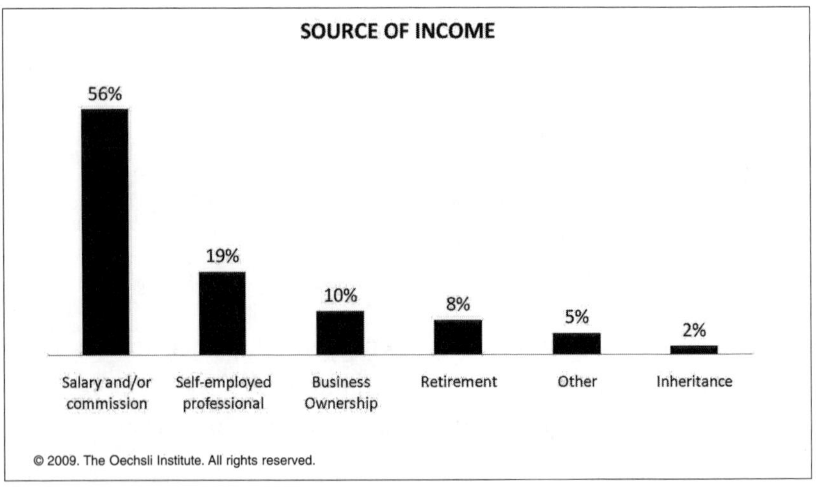

The affluent are desperately seeking "go-to" financial coordinators, because they need help with all *4 Key Motivators.* They want *you* to become their financial guardian.

Spiritual Health

"I need to start going back to church/temple."
"I need to get more in touch with my spiritual side."
"I need to give more to my church / temple."
"When the time comes, how do I distribute the estate?"
"Pop's lived a good life; I know I'll see him in heaven."

Most of your affluent clients have been exposed to death in some form. It might be a stretch to link your team to this key motivator, but think in terms of death benefits, funeral arrangements and tithing. If your team is *really* doing its job as a "go-to" financial coordinator, your work impacts each of these *4 Key Affluent Motivators.*

Who Do They Trust?

To develop elite teams that consistently acquire affluent clients in the U.S. and around the world, you must build trust and consistently deliver the goods. The most successful financial services professionals and financial teams develop rock-solid track records, and therefore, rock-solid referral bases founded on the trusted friends, family and associates of clients.

That's it.

There are no shortcuts. As shown in the chart below, most professionals are struggling to build the trust they so desperately need.

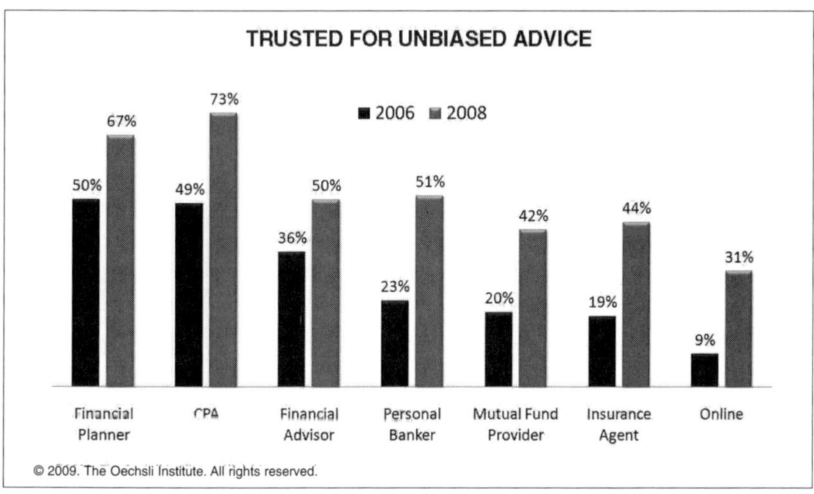

A financial team can usually beat a "lone wolf," but it must first prove that it's an effective team and promote itself through word of mouth. No duo (or trio) of fast-talking salesmen will beat a solo practitioner by double- or triple-teaming prospects—handing out glossy brochures and making clichéd elevator speeches—unless trusted friends and family members first vouch for them.

All things being equal, would you buy a classic, restored 1965 Mustang convertible from a pimply-faced teenager who advertised in the local newspaper, or from a reputable antique auto dealer who'd been recommended by every collector in your county? When big money is involved, the answer is obvious.

Put simply, if you want to work with the affluent, an elite team affords you the best opportunity to attract, service, and develop loyal affluent clients. You will earn more money by leveraging the synergy of 1 + 1 = 3, 4 or even 5. This is true of all elite teams, though it involves hard work. It's extremely difficult to provide the right expertise, Ritz Carlton service and FedEx efficiency by going solo.

To be an attractive solutions provider for the multi-dimensional aspects of the affluent family's financial affairs, it takes an elite team.

Summary

- Affluent investors want a "go-to" financial coordinator or financial team to manage *every* aspect of their increasingly complex financial affairs.
- When making purchase decisions, over 65% of survey respondents said the opinions of immediate family members and trusted friends had a very significant impact on deciding where to look for options.
- Always keep in mind the 4 Key Affluent Motivators: Personal Health, Family Health, Spiritual Health and (especially) Financial Health.
- Building trust develops word-of-mouth referrals, which is critical to maintaining a steady stream of prospects in your "pipeline."
- It is very difficult to coordinate every aspect of an affluent family's financial affairs as a sole practitioner.
- Elite Financial Teams have a distinct advantage.

2

Sobering Realities, Tremendous Opportunities

> *The majority of teams in the financial services industry are loose confederations of financial professionals, rather than elite teams.*
>
> —Factoid, Financial Team Research

Bringing a group of competent individuals together as a team is no simple task. Logic tells us that success cannot occur overnight. Even a quick review of our research shows that teams of all types tend to evolve through predictable stages of development. As I mentioned in the Introduction, a widely accepted framework for describing this journey is the *Forming, Storming, Norming* and *Performing* model of team development developed by Dr. Bruce W. Tuckman at Ohio State University.

In part, The Oechsli Institute's research was undertaken to determine how financial teams progress through Dr. Tuckman's stages of development. Our interest was sparked by a dramatic increase in the number of financial teams in the financial services industry—teams engineered (in theory) to capture an ever larger share of the affluent market.

Because of the large pools of assets involved when financial advisors form a team, these groups have received considerable attention within the world of financial services. And a simple, but significant, truth has emerged. True financial teams, ones that excel in attracting, servicing and retaining affluent clients, are in great demand. But as our research indicates, such teams are a rarity. Financial teams are out-performing individual financial advisors in affluent client acquisition, but they still have a lot of room for improvement.

All of this brings us to the key question: Is there a formula that a financial team can apply to accelerate their development through Dr. Tuckman's stages? Is there a clear path to follow? Can a team's current stage of development be identified, analyzed, benchmarked and then given a course of action? The purpose behind our Elite Financial Team research was to find answers to those and other vital questions related to financial team success.

Again, most of what we read about financial teams focuses on the 17% that have achieved the highest levels of performance. What we are *not* hearing is how they got there, or why the other 83% are struggling to get there.

In the chart below you can see the significant differences between teams in the *Forming* and *Storming* stages and those in the *Norming* and *Performing* stages. Please note the subtle difference between teams in the *Norming* and *Performing* stages. This reveals why the quest for elite status should be the objective of every team.

Let's revisit the four stages of team development in more depth.

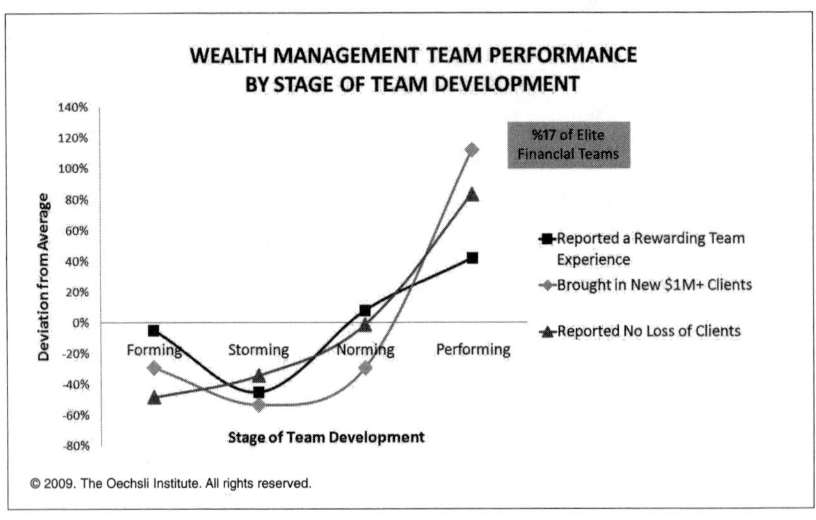

Forming Stage—12% of our respondents fall into this category. At this stage, there is both excitement and anxiety. People are cautiously optimistic. Individual roles and responsibilities are unclear, and team members are often guarded in their interactions. Team members are totally dependent on their Team Leader for guidance.

Not enough time and attention is devoted to this stage, but it is unquestionably the most important stage. You have to get the right people onboard, for the right reasons, with the right work ethic, the right integrity (total), the right core competencies, and a compatible goal focus—both business and personal. Whew! It's no wonder so many teams blow through this critical stage of development. It requires a lot of soul searching. It's a lot of work.

Following is a checklist to help you take the proper steps in this stage, since it's here that most would-be teams fail to exercise proper due-diligence.

Forming Checklist

1. **Trust.** You need a 360-degree circle of trust, meaning you must have complete trust in your partner(s), and they must have complete trust in you. This is the integrity component essential to a team's long-term success.
2. **Compatibility.** Although trust is essential, you also must be able to get along in a high-pressure business environment. This is much different than enjoying each other's company socially. The following graph is taken from our 2007 and 2009 studies on financial teams. We asked these teams, "How important is it for team members to share common values for work effort, work quality and client service?" As you can see quite clearly, what teams consider extremely important is not always connected with their day-to-day reality.

   That said, 96% of teams found these shared values to be "very" to "extremely" important, however, few truly take this into consideration when forming a team.

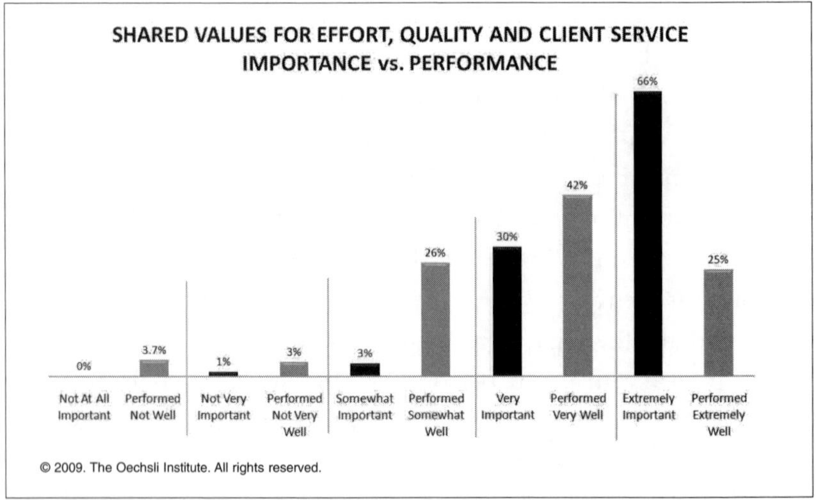

3. **Work Ethic.** Whenever one partner perceives that he or she is working harder than the other, resentment surfaces that will ultimately lead to conflict and destroy the team. Everyone must agree on the desired work ethic prior to forming.
4. **Competency.** This should go without saying, but all team members must be fully capable of performing well in their areas of expertise. History is a fairly good indicator. For instance, if a partner has acquired very few clients over the past 12 months, he or she will probably struggle in marketing the team—a.k.a., Rainmaking.
5. **Comprehensive Business Plan.** Each partner must agree on the team's vision –the long-range goals, ideal client, number of ideal clients, assets, revenue, services provided, etc. This is essential for creating a "critical path" that the team will follow as it grows.
6. **Clear & Unified Goals.** Each partner has to buy-in to annual team goals, meaning they must subjugate personal goals to the collective goals.
7. **Clear Roles & Responsibilities.** Every team member should have a clear role and delegated areas of responsibility prior to forming.

8. **Partner Contribution Clarity.** Each partner should have a clear understanding of his/her individual contribution to the team's annual goals. Procedures should be in place for making partner compensation adjustments if one partner . . .
—Exceeds Individual Contribution Targets, or
—Falls Behind Individual Contribution Targets.
9. **Client Segmentation.** Before forming the team, partners must agree on how they will segment their current client base. Whether it is "A" and "B" or "Platinum" and "Gold" clients, they should agree on the appropriate levels of service to be delivered to each segment.
10. **Wealth Management Services Provided.** Partners should agree on a client-centric process that is consistent for every client fitting a certain profile—i.e., "Platinum" versus "Gold" clients. Otherwise, they run the risk of letting each partner handle clients differently, which creates challenges in Practice Management.
11. **Compensation.** A bonus structure for non-partner team members (support personnel) should be agreed on in advance. This should be based on team growth and individual contributions.
12. **Individual Performance Reviews.** Partners need to agree on who will conduct these, how they will be conducted, and when the performance reviews of support personnel will occur.
13. **Basic Team Operations.** Obtain agreement on weekly team meetings, phone coverage, office hours, etc.
14. **Partner Performance Reviews.** Team partners must be held to the same level of performance accountability (if not greater) as the team's support personnel. Senior partners should review junior partners, equal partners must review each other, and senior partners must allow their performance to be reviewed by junior partners.
15. **Team Performance Reviews.** Schedule an annual retreat or similar type of offsite meeting, attended by every team member, to review the past year's achievements, reinforce team accountability for achieving goals, make necessary adjustments, and agree on the upcoming year's goals.

It doesn't take long to realize that, done properly, this *Forming* stage requires a lot of work, which is why some steps are frequently skipped. This is a mistake that you must avoid. If you determine that your team is stuck in either the Storming or Norming stage, working through this checklist is a worthwhile exercise. I've included a *Team Forming Assessment* in the appendix for this purpose.

Storming Stage*—17% of our respondents fall into this category.* Shortly after the excitement of forming a team wears off, reality sinks in. Now, everyone must learn to work together. This is the stage where team members frequently begin challenging each other, and strained relations emerge. They struggle through their differences, and decisions do not come easily. The Team Leader's responsibility is to resolve conflicts and focus the team's efforts toward the next stage. No matter how successful a financial team becomes, it must pass through this stage. The secret is passing through it quickly.

Because so many teams skip the Forming stage exercise, naively assuming they will somehow come together, the *Storming* stage can come as a real shock. Often, the hard reality of *Storming* hits team members like a whack on the side of the head.

However, even teams that devote the time and effort to forming properly will have to endure this stage of team development. It's inevitable. The secret is to be prepared, since *Storming* is a natural stage in learning how to get along in close quarters. An effective Team Leader recognizes this, and works hard to quickly steer the team through this period into the *Norming* stage. The following are basic guidelines to help your team accelerate through this stage:

- Expect interpersonal differences
- Proactively resolve conflict without making it personal
- Proactively promote teamwork and harmony
- Work to strengthen interpersonal relationships
- Emphasize individual and team accountability
- Reinforce goal focus

By paying attention to the aforementioned, you will hasten your team's journey through this difficult stage of development. You will have created a basic harmony within your team and entered into what Dr. Tuckman refers to as the *Norming* stage.

Norming Stage—40% of our respondents fall into this category. During this period, team members learn to work in harmony. Individual roles and responsibilities become clear and accepted. Team members work hard to reach consensus when making decisions. Commitment and unity are strong, and team members are not as dependent on the guidance and direction of their Team Leader. The team experiences cohesion, and begins to provide a complete array of wealth management services.

Financial teams in the *Norming Stage* often give the appearance of elite status, but *actual* elite status still eludes them. This is a dangerous time, because if teams fail to move to higher ground (the *Performing Stage)*, they may fall back into the *Storming Stage.* We refer to this as the *Storming-Norming trap.*

Effective Team Leaders recognize that getting along (Norming) is merely a platform on which accountability (collective and individual) for reaching team goals can be enforced. Everyone needs to pull his weight. If this doesn't happen, team members will eventually become disgruntled and start bickering (the usual topics are money and work ethic). Suddenly, the team is Storming again.

It's important to accelerate through this stage with the same urgency as you sped through the *Storming* stage. By paying attention to the following, you will drastically lessen the probability of falling into the Storming-Norming trap.

- Make certain each team member's roles and responsibilities are clear and fully accepted.
- Continually communicate how roles and responsibilities are linked to team goals.
- Stimulate contrarian ideas that are linked to growth and improvement.
- Reinforce a strong focus on team goals.
- Expand wealth management services.
- Commit revised policies and procedures to writing.

- Emphasize complete individual accountability.
- Instill accountability into weekly team meetings.
- Inspire and direct team members to your vision (long-range business plan).

The importance of expeditiously leading your team through this stage can't be overemphasized. Lingering in a state of workplace harmony for too long is inherently dangerous. When this occurs, your team may easily fall into the *Storming-Norming trap.*

The Storming-Norming Trap: A Closer Look

Few teams are aware that they have cycled backward into the *Storming* stage until it's too late. In my experience, many teams survive one rotation through this cycle on their way to the *Performing* stage, but few weather a second rotation. Hence, I have witnessed many ugly divorces. I recall one where my services were asked for in the midst of a team's second *Storming-Norming* rotation.

Jim and Larry had developed a very successful team. They had partnered for more than six years before serious problems developed. But something occurred that changed the dynamic between the two equal partners: success.

For three of those six years, I was intimately involved with the team, including support personnel, compensation agreements, delegated roles and responsibilities, and (of course) Rainmaking. Both Jim and Larry had mastered the art of Rainmaking. They could sell the relationship, introduce the team, bring in the serious money, and penetrate their wealthy clients' centers-of-influence. Larry once said, "We have the best job in the world. All we do is hang out with our wealthiest clients, play with them on their yachts and holiday homes, manage their money, and get introduced to their friends. It doesn't get any better than that."

I agreed, but then I committed a team-coaching faux pas: I assumed they no longer needed my guidance, and told them to call if they ever needed further advice.

Two years later, I received a call from Jim. "Larry's no longer working. I've got the most expensive partner in the industry. He's making over $1 million a year, comes in at 10 a.m., and leaves every day at 4 p.m. Since we last talked, he hasn't brought in any new business, while I've busted my butt traveling up and down the East Coast to bring in $80 million dollars—which I *resent* splitting with him!"

Storm clouds were not just on the horizon. Jim and Larry were already engulfed by them.

As it turned out, Larry was no longer committed to their long-range goal of being a $10 million team with over $1 billion in assets. All of his financial needs were met, his children were grown and raising their own families, so Larry wanted to slow down and spend more time with his wife. (I was envious when he explained this to me.) Problem was: he never communicated his change of heart to Jim, who was still goal-focused and had no intention of slowing down.

Their disagreement started with work ethic, and progressed to money. Jim wanted Larry to resume his Rainmaking activities to bring in his share of new money. Larry thought he'd earned the right to do whatever he wanted.

I was called in to mediate.

Long story short, it was a grueling process. Each partner said things about the other that would never be forgiven. Larry was accused of working part-time and being untrustworthy. Jim was accused of being a womanizer, playing the role of the rich and famous (and having expenses to match).

Since neither was prepared to break up the team, an agreement was reached: Larry would lower his partnership percentage and, though he would not travel for new business, he would do a better job of managing their local wealthy relationships. Jim would still function as the Rainmaker, but would now receive an extra 10 percent of the business. In the end, however, this agreement was as effective as a band-aid over a gunshot wound.

In less than three months, they were back in the Storming stage, and this time it was *really* ugly. They divorced. Not only did they break up the team, they fought over clients, bad-mouthed each other, and engaged in numerous acts of immature and unprofessional behavior.

Just one example of how teams rarely survive a second trip through *Storming-Norming* land.

I learned a valuable lesson as a team coach: no matter how successful a team becomes, basic issues need to be addressed in a periodic manner—before they get out of control. From that point forward, I've insisted that teams conduct quarterly reviews and hold annual retreats, which I detail later in this book.

Performing Stage*—31% of our respondents fall into this category (but only 17% qualify as* "elite status"*).* Here, team goals are being realized. The team clearly knows the direction in which it's going and why. Members work together to achieve goals, strengthen relationships and support each other's efforts. Team members are able to work equally well as individuals, in small groups and as a team. At this stage, the Team Leader essentially delegates, coordinates and participates with the team.

For financial teams this stage is a "tweener." The team is growing, there is accountability for performance, but it's not yet firing on all cylinders. It could slip back into the *Norming stage* if leadership is not vigilant about ensuring that everyone remains totally focused on the team's goals. Our research indicates that over 50% of the teams in the *Performing* stage are led effectively; these teams will have a much better chance of reaching the coveted status of *elite.*

A Team Leader should never take elite status for granted, and must consistently remind members that ongoing growth and improvement is the norm. During this stage, an effective leader will make certain that:

- Job satisfaction is high, and a focus on results is equally strong.
- Every member continues striving to achieve the team's goals.
- Each member is committed to ongoing improvement of self and team.

- Accountability remains strong in all areas.
- Communication is open, honest and clear.
- Team meetings are consistent, effective and productive.
- The Team Leader continues to direct, inspire, and solve problems.

Elite *—Only 17% of our respondents fall into this category.* More than half of survey respondents in the *Performing Stage* excel in every aspect of attracting, servicing and retaining affluent clients. They consistently acquire more new $1-million-plus relationships than other teams or solo advisors, they also develop specific annual acquisition targets. They bring in serious levels of new assets, and achieve consistent revenue growth. The team provides a full array of wealth management services, with Ritz Carlton-level service and FedEx-level efficiency. Elite status is reached when the team generates specific results for affluent client acquisition, client retention and team member career satisfaction.

This stage of development is every team's dream, but few are able to reach it. Yes, it *is* leader-directed, but it requires that everyone pulls together. The focus of this book is to accelerate your development into an Elite Financial Team.

Let me introduce you to the Foundations Team by letting you observe one of their meetings. As you'll quickly notice, Hollywood couldn't have cast a more perfect elite team. They are perfectly suited for attracting, servicing and developing loyal affluent clients.

But it wasn't always like this . . .

The Foundations Team

Imagine being a fly-on-the wall at the weekly meeting of the *Foundations Financial Team*. You observe six well-dressed financial professionals arriving a few minutes early to the conference room, one carrying an overflowing tray of Starbucks. As they gather around the conference table, reports have been prepared and are waiting for them. By the time the clock strikes 8 AM, everyone is seated, has read the report of the previous week's accomplishments, and has reviewed the meeting agenda.

You are witnessing a financial team that has reached the elite stage of team development.

These six professionals, from the Team Leader to the administrative assistant to the junior advisor, are all goal-focused. All are committed to performing at a high level, and each is clear about his or her role in making that happen. Everyone takes personal pride in his or her contribution. Being a part of this elite team is a rewarding experience.

Here's how their meeting goes . . .

- Ben, the team's Practice Manager, opens the meeting with an overview of the agenda and a review of the previous week.
- Chuck, the team's Leader and Rainmaker, reports that he had five meetings last week, and brought in $6 million from one new relationship, and that there is now over $60 million in the team's pipeline.
- Mary, the team's CFP, reports on the financial plans she has completed for upcoming review meetings, and asks about the follow-up needs of the new $6 million dollar client.
- George, a CPA who oversees tax strategies for the team, reviews tax-saving opportunities for six current affluent clients.
- Gerry, a junior advisor three years out of graduate school, reports on the golf outing he's been working on that will involve four clients and four of their friends (prospects).
- Jane, the administrative assistant, reviews what is pending and what needs signatures, and discusses a problem that's been recurring. The issue is discussed by the group until a solution is determined.
- Chuck then closes the meeting by outlining the team's schedule for the week—client meetings, rainmaking activities, and expectations.

This is a financial team in the *Performing Stage* of team development. Actually, it's in the elite phase of the *Performing Stage*. But it wasn't always like this, and no one feels better about the transformation than Ben and Chuck. They are the only original team members.

It took Chuck 15 years of disciplined, goal-focused effort to become a $1.5 million solo producer. He knew that in order to improve his ability to attract, service, and retain affluent clients he needed to form a financial team. Ben, a failed trainee who loved the business, was his first hire. Ben's role was not to prospect, but to produce reports and handle some of the more complex research assignments. Ben excelled at both. That was five years ago, and they have since zigzagged through the stages of team development to where they are today.

The Right People Make the Best Teams

When it comes to building teams, I look to Jim Collins, author of the bestseller *Good to Great*, because he makes this important point: "The old adage that 'People are your most important asset' is wrong. People are not your most important asset. The *right* people are."

Selecting the *right people* for your team is a critical first step for Team Leaders. If a job could talk, it would clearly define the knowledge, hard skills, people skills, behavior and culture needed for superior performance. Through our research, we've been able to benchmark the financial advisor and support personnel roles as they relate to a team. Without getting into too much detail, every prospective team member must be vetted using three key criteria.

1. ***Will they perform the role?*** Here, you want to determine the personal attributes, attitude and cognitive ability needed to perform the role.
2. ***Why will they perform?*** This area is where you need to determine their personal values. Will they perform for your team?
3. ***How will they perform?*** An individual's behavioral traits need to match those of the role. Once you determine that someone is

compatible with the role, you need to make certain that each team member has a *hunger* for elite status.

Bottom line: If you want to *build* an elite team, look for team members who have a *hunger* for achieving elite status! This is the first, best step toward building an Elite Financial Team.

Assessing Prospective Team Members

As noted earlier, Jim Collins stresses that when you hire good people (get the right people on the bus/team), you accelerate your chances for success. It doesn't matter whether the individual member has experience in a particular area. What matters is that the prospective team member is willing to learn, accept whatever role is necessary at the time, has a strong work ethic, and displays integrity and brains. Put simply: an honest, hard-working neophyte can be trained to become a better practice manager than the experienced veteran who is lazy and dishonest. The following graph illustrates the importance of getting the right people on your team. We asked teams, "How important is it for team members to subordinate their personal goals to team goals?"

Too often, I've seen Team Leaders hire or promote junior partners with fatal flaws—putting the wrong people on the bus. They were hired

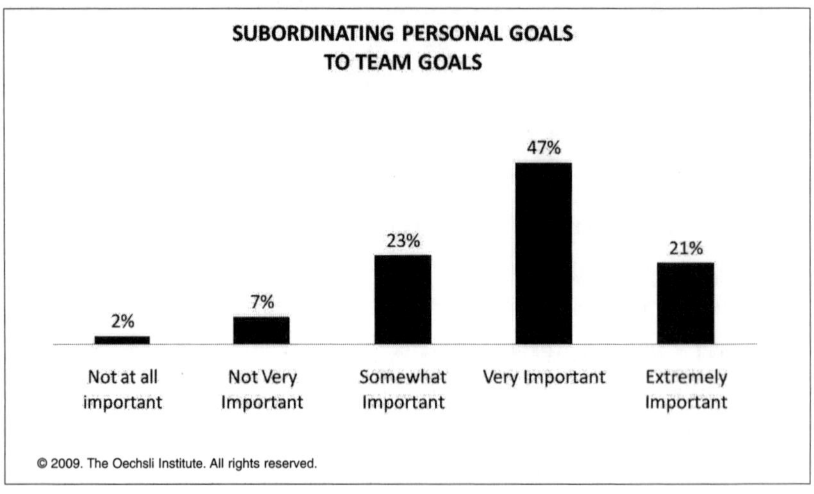

because they had bucket-loads of industry experience, so it was mistakenly assumed that they'd need very little training. Big mistake!

Assessment Tools and Techniques

Assessment tools like the Myers-Briggs Personality Type Indicator (and many different behavioral profiles) are commonly used to screen applicants. When used properly, they can be quite helpful, but they cannot guarantee that you'll put the right person on the bus. They need to be complemented with traditional screening tools, including thorough background checks, to discover the "real story" of past performance.

Of course, this is easier said than done.

I once hired an assistant after she failed our assessment (according to my interpretation), but because I liked her, she interviewed well and she displayed a professional demeanor, I ignored the assessment tool. I should have had my team members tape a sign reading "KICK ME" on my back. Within two weeks, I had to let her go. Not only was she incapable of doing the job on a cognitive and emotional level, she pulled everyone else off track. She was a "motor mouth" who never stopped blabbing.

My next hire was an ace, according to the assessments, which I even reviewed with the team that had created them. Everyone's call was, "Hire her!"

I was leery, so I started her on a per-project basis. Although she performed extremely well, just as the assessment predicted, I still wasn't comfortable with her, but I was getting pressure from everyone to hire her on a permanent basis. So I did . . . very slowly. Within two months, however, it became apparent that she did not like the financial services industry. In fact, she resented people with money and resented people who make their living servicing people with money.

I had to let her go.

Even the best assessment tools are no substitute for your intuition.

Listen to the Pros

Many CEOs, business writers and academics point to sports teams as paragons for building a winning business team. What's amazing, however, is how few businesspeople actually practice what their heroes' preach. Many "pillars of our economy" seem to worship coaches like Lou Holtz and Mike Ditka, but ignore the best practices of these role models.

That's too bad, because every leader throughout history is an encyclopedia of learning—whether Julius Caesar, Mike Ditka, Napoleon or Abraham Lincoln. To really learn anything from such figures, business leaders must know what to look for in their heroes' leadership styles. This includes factors such as:

- How they handled people.
- How they responded to problems / crises.
- How they communicated their visions.
- Their personal commitments to their causes.
- Their work ethics.
- Their attitudes.
- Their goal-focus.

Most people fail to learn the prime lessons of history, because . . . well . . . most people are not students of history or high achievers. What's more, leadership lessons are not explicitly taught in school. That's why, as a coach to financial service providers, I ask many "students" to select a hero—a role model from history or their personal lives—and then I walk them through an IQ (Inner Quality) / SQ (School Quality) exercise. The exercise goes like this:

- Identify your hero. (Let's say, Abe Lincoln.)
- List all the qualities you admire, all the qualities that you attribute to his greatness, as well as his achievements. (Let's say hard work, integrity, self-taught, highly disciplined, persistent, resilient, goal-focused, problem solver, courageous, sense of humor, etc.)
- Next, I ask participants to label each quality as either an IQ (an inner quality—one learned through life's lessons) or an SQ (a

school quality—one taught in an actual schoolroom, tested and graded on).

- Typically, more than 90% of leadership qualities are rated as IQ, and the figure often reaches 100%. In other words, inner qualities rule!

The main lesson is that we are not taught how to achieve success, as leaders, in our structured educational system. Team Leaders and successful financial professionals are not being taught how to develop and lead elite teams in the classroom.

The Rush to Build Teams

Over the last 10 years, there has been an incredible rush to build financial teams in the financial services industry.

Why did this all start?

A number of factors have fueled the rush.

First, many senior financial professionals had a large client base, controlled large sums of assets, and their firms were concerned about succession planning (following retirement or death), believing that having a junior advisor work with a senior advisor would help protect the assets and lessen the likelihood of a large producer moving to another firm. (The thinking is that because teams have more moving parts in terms of more people, they are harder to transport from one firm to another.)

Second, the affluent are looking to a solutions provider for the multi-dimensional aspects of their families' financial affairs. This is extremely difficult to provide as a sole practitioner. Because the affluent recognize this, teams have come into fashion. After all, this was the approach that Goldman Sachs took to working with wealthy families. Unfortunately, it often became more of a marketing tactic: "We'll market ourselves as a team and get more affluent clients."

Our research is quite clear: the affluent want comprehensive wealth management; a true solutions provider to coordinate every aspect of their family's financial affairs.

The flaw in this marketing tactic is obvious: only 17% of teams are performing at high levels (true solutions providers, delivering comprehensive wealth management). And as I've already indicated, most so-called teams are merely loose confederations of financial professionals playing at being financial teams—i.e., pretenders. *The affluent see right through this!*

Ready, Fire, Aim!

Many teams form hastily, without the necessary planning, due-diligence and hard pre-work. A few years ago, a leading financial services company was so focused on teams that it promoted "Team Formation" as one of the key metrics that branch managers would be bonused on. The result? You guessed it. Because compensation drives results, teams were formed, but . . . "These arranged marriages were destined to fail." (This is the analogy given by one of the firm's senior financial advisors.) And, since the financial services industry often follows the leader, once this firm started leading the field in "quantity" of teams, other firms followed their team formation approach. Everyone seemed to agree that is was easier for a team to service the affluent. Therefore, teaming must make good sense.

Also, because Goldman Sachs has both panache and cache, and launched the whole team sales concept in the financial world, most advisors wanted to copy them, thinking this would jumpstart their marketing efforts.

Other financial advisors simply rushed to build teams out of convenience. "I'll cover for you when you're out, and you'll cover for me." Obviously, these teams formed for the wrong reasons, and did so in a slap-dash "ready, fire, aim" fashion. Toss a few FA's together in an office, add a pinch of support personnel, stir in a quick mission statement, and there's your winning recipe!

Recent conference calls with two major financial institutions tell the story. Both had reviewed one of our research reports on financial teams. Both had a directive from senior management to the training department: Develop a model for successful teams. One firm had approximately 800 teams; the other wasn't sure. The questions I was asked tell the real story:

> *Question:* "What firm's are doing the best job in developing Elite Financial Teams?"
>
> *My Answer:* "Our research is clear on this. Elite teams, regardless of firm or whether they are independent, have more in common with each other than they do with other teams at their firm or independent channel."

The response was a muted "Oh." Apparently, my answer was either too complex or unwelcome. Their mission was to find out what was working, customize it, and use it to train teams in their firm. Alas, there is no cookie-cutter approach.

After explaining the *Forming-Storming-Norming-Performing* stages of development, and what our research uncovered about the challenges in the *Forming* stage (and the dangers of the *Storming-Norming* trap), one caller's follow-up question was even more revealing.

> *Question:* "Which firm is doing a better job at the *Forming* stage?"
>
> *My Answer:* "None. This stage requires a lot of work, due-diligence, getting the right people on board doing the right tasks, for the right reasons—all linked to the goals of the team."

The message for anyone who's currently on a team or forming a team is simple: there is no cookie-cutter approach—just as there is no cookie-cutter approach to raising a functional family. And teams are a business family.

Defining Purpose

Before deciding whether to assemble a group of financial advisors and support personnel into a team, you must first define the team's purpose. And the main purpose of a financial team should be attracting, servicing and developing loyal affluent clients. From the client perspective, your purpose is to provide comprehensive wealth management services, offering Ritz Carlton-level service with FedEx-style efficiency. From an internal team perspective, you also need a serious commitment to growth.

What *Not* to Do.

Let me take you through an example of what happens when a financial services firm develops an objective for management compensation that is directly attached to the number of solo advisors who form or join teams.

One morning, while I was "on the road" in Washington DC, I received a call from a veteran advisor who was producing $2.5 million a year and had $450 million in assets under management. This 62-year-old gentleman solicited my advice about forming a team with a buddy, a 63-year-old, $3.2 million producer with $600 million in assets under management.

They had worked in the same office for decades. They knew each other, liked each other, and were afraid of losing their top-producer status in the office. In effect, they were feeling *loads* of pressure, albeit indirect, to form a team. If they did, they would instantly become the biggest revenue-producing team in the office (whereas they had previously enjoyed the #1 and #2 slots as individuals).

In response to his inquiry, I asked him five simple questions that I always ask of anyone interested in forming a financial team:

- ✓ Do you trust your prospective partner? (Yes.)
- ✓ Do your work ethics mesh? (He wasn't sure how hard either of them wanted to work at their ages.)
- ✓ Are your areas of competence compatible? (They were both stockbrokers, not wealth managers, and had different opinions on investments.)
- ✓ Can you both buy in to a long-range business plan? (They didn't have a business plan.)
- ✓ Are you both willing to do the "heavy lifting" associated with building an effective team? (The answer was "no.")

This little exercise of due-diligence in the *Forming* stage was the end of that potential team. The veteran solo advisor realized that not only would the team have been a disaster, it would have probably killed both of them (literally).

The beginnings of the Foundations Team illustrate how easy it is to get completely derailed on your way to elite status. There are numerous performance-damaging traps, and this team fell into a number of them. It was only because of the radical changes made by the Team Leader (within himself) that they were eventually able to continue their journey. Let's visit a time when they nearly fell apart.

The Foundations Team . . .
In the Beginning

Within six months of hiring Ben, two young aggressive junior advisors approached Chuck and sold him on joining his young team and functioning as the "marketing department." They wanted to be the team leader, responsible for new business development—and "selling" the team. Everyone was excited, especially Chuck, because he envisioned that now, with his two eager "marketing execs", the team would quickly reach the 5 million dollar high-water mark. Shortly after that, he also hired an administrative assistant.

Foundations Team Storming — Over the next few months, the *Foundations Financial Team* almost ceased to exist. Not a day went by without conflict among the five team members. The two junior financial advisors spent more time trying to undermine each other and run off Ben than they did bringing in new business. The team's young assistant was attractive, but had minimal office experience. Her modus operandi was to offset her incompetence by flirting with Chuck.

It all came to a head during a team meeting. (I know this because I was there.) Here's a snapshot of what occurred:

- Minutes before the meeting, each junior advisor cornered me (alone) to express his displeasure with the others, especially Ben. Both insisted Ben should be fired.
- Nobody was sure where Sally (the administrative assistant) was, because she was running late—as usual.
- Chuck was getting anxious and irritated with Sally's tardiness. My being there didn't help.

- The meeting finally started at 9 AM (it was scheduled for 8:30 A.M.).
- Chuck began by proudly displaying the business plan, roles and responsibilities, policies and procedures, metrics score system, etc. that he had drawn up. Looking around, I could see that no one except Ben seemed to care.
- The junior advisors said nice things about the team and Chuck's leadership.
- Ben and Sally were quiet.
- I asked a performance question: "How many new $1 million relationships has the team acquired over the past 12 months?" There was dead silence — until the storm hit!
- Chuck slammed his fist on the conference table, and shouted a profanity along the lines of "We all suck!" He then pointed to his two junior advisors, challenging them to prove their worth over the next three months—or else.
- The meeting ended with Chuck announcing that he was going to become the team's Rainmaker, and vowing he could bring in more business than his two junior advisors combined. Sally was terminated three weeks later. Within three months, the two junior advisors had departed, each of his own volition.

Many financial advisors will read through these Stages and their descriptions and mistakenly assume they can leapfrog from *Forming* to *Performing*. After all, they reason, "We were successful as individuals, so we'll simply pool our talents and become even more successful."

This is simply naïve, as anyone who has ever been on a team will attest. You know the old approach, "We'll just pull together two or more senior financial advisors, add a junior or two, mix in a few assistants, and send out some flyers to announce our new financial team." That's what the *Foundations Financial Team* did initially, but it didn't work. Yet, somehow they regrouped (revisited the *Forming Stage)* and made the necessary changes to build the dream team that Chuck and Ben had envisioned. The question is: what did they do? What is required to take a financial team to elite status?

Chuck, the Foundation's Team Leader radically changed his leadership style. First and foremost, he became more of a hands-on leader and a source of ongoing inspiration for team members. Second, he took over the role of the team's primary Rainmaker. It was amazing to watch the overall accountability improve as a result. And finally, he made certain problems were handled before they escalated into major issues.

This hands-on approach was a major departure from Chuck's previous role as Team Leader. Every team member underwent an exhaustive assessment process to determine his or her ability to perform their assigned role, to determine their motivation to perform for his team, and finally to determine how each individual would perform within the framework of an elite team. It took nearly six months for Chuck to get the right people on board, but once everyone was in place, they blew through the *Storming* and *Norming* stages of development. Within two months they were hitting stride as an elite team. The first challenge for any Team Leader is selecting the right team members. In Chuck's case, he made a number of mistakes. The question is, did he select the wrong people—or did he have them doing the wrong things—or both?

Role clarity is important, but roles can and need to be adjusted at times to meet changing situations and challenges. Something else was missing in the group Chuck initially assembled, and it was that "something else" that became strikingly evident in our research. We found that a direct correlation exists between how rewarding our respondents said their team experience was and the quality of the team's performance. The higher a team's performance, the more rewarding each individual's role. This strong correlation between rewarding experience and elite status tells us a lot about the kind of team we need to build.

What *to* Do

An unwavering truth about elite teams is their unusual capacity to both plan and execute continuous growth. Business development is a two-sided coin. On one side is careful planning (the business plan), while the other features relentless execution. A team needs both. Any financial team that is not in "growth mode" is vulnerable. The old adage, "if you're not growing, you're dying," is a mantra confirmed up by our research. Carefully planned and executed business development is at the core of all elite teams.

Many teams have some form of business plan, with a good number having well-developed written plans. What separates the high performers from the rest is their ability to execute! The "top guns" adhere to their plans. It becomes their critical path. From new client acquisition targets to fully monetizing existing clients, everything is linked to the successful execution of the business plan.

Upgrading existing clients is really about repositioning your services. It's very important for a financial team to serve as the solutions provider for the multi-dimensional aspects of clients' financial affairs. This is a "win-win," because whenever a team performs this function, it is more likely to monetize the relationship.

Affluent client loyalty is linked hand-to-glove to business development. This truism is at the core of all elite team success. Because the affluent use word-of-mouth influence as a primary tool for serious decision making, loyal affluent clients are the focal point of any successful business development effort. Every elite team, like every Rainmaker, understands and effectively manages these relationships. And they manage them at all levels.

Every member of an Elite Financial Team assumes personal responsibility for delivering five-star service; every client contact is deemed important, and team members continually look for new ways to surprise and delight clients. Again, one of the key differences between elite teams and the rest is the ability of the former to combine consistent delivery of high-level service with business development.

Client loyalty and business development are at the core of an Elite Financial Team. And this arena is directly linked to both the practice management and wealth management processes. Client loyalty is the result of positive long-term behavior, whereas client satisfaction is a short-term emotion. Every team member impacts client loyalty, whether he or she is solving a problem quickly or surprising and delighting loyal affluent clients.

When it comes to wealth management, the financial services industry's PR machine has elevated the decibel level to where it seems like every financial institution and every financial professional is virtually the same. And if one were to believe everything he heard at face value, one would assume that every team, every financial professional, every financial firm—big or small—delivers the full array of wealth management services.

As we know all too well, this hype isn't remotely linked to reality.

What is the reality?

It's that Elite Financial Teams deliver the goods. They understand what the affluent are looking for, they have invested the time and money to acquire the necessary expertise, and they have developed a process for delivering financial solutions to their clients.

The "tremendous opportunity" mentioned in this chapter's title refers to the advantages that the elite team can bring to both its clients and itself. Because there are so few teams meeting client needs and expectations, the truly elite team—"the real deal"—can easily scoop up new business from their many dysfunctional rivals, rivals merely playing at being true financial teams.

There can be no mistake about it: elite teams are the future of the financial services industry. The affluent demand the best, they deserve the best, and they will ultimately get the best.

Summary

- True financial teams, ones that excel in attracting, servicing and retaining affluent clients, are in great demand. But our research indicates that such teams are a rarity.
- All teams follow the progression of Forming, Storming, Norming and Performing, but the most successful ones pass through the early stages quickly, thanks to inspired and sensible leadership.
- The Storming-Norming trap is real. Every team needs to be aware and continue their focus on growth. Successful teams need to learn a lesson from Jim and Larry.
- Many financial teams form for the wrong reasons—out of convenience or because individuals are pressured by management to create teams. A dysfunctional team is worse than no team at all.

- More due-diligence is required in the *Forming* stage; the *Forming Checklist* is a must. Consider the investment of time and energy as preventative medicine.
- Every team that is not currently in the Performing stage would benefit from working through the *Forming Checklist.*
- If you want the right people on your team, you need to have answers to three questions; Will they perform the role? Why will they perform? How will they perform?
- Although many affluent prospects believe the industry hype that "all financial teams are alike," elite teams excel at delivering the goods by carefully adhering to carefully crafted business plans.
- The affluent are looking for precisely what Elite Financial Teams deliver.

SECTION II

The 5 Components of an Elite Financial Team

As elite teams progressed from the *Performing* stage into elite status, we identified 15 statistically significant performance factors they all had in common. It was these performance factors that enabled me to create our five-part, Elite Financial Team model. A direct link was established between the results these teams were able to achieve in terms of:

- Number of new affluent clients acquired,
- Retention of affluent clients,
- New assets acquired from new and existing clients,
- Percentage of revenues that were fee-based, and
- Percentage of production increase,

and these 15 performance factors.

In the upcoming chapters, I will explain how these performance factors are distributed throughout our team model. I want you to be able to adopt whatever will help your team's performance. Collectively, these factors are responsible for the growth of the team—for achieving elite status.

3

Team Leadership

(Performance Factors 1, 2 & 3)

Effective Team Leaders inspire and direct performance.

—Factoid, Financial Team Research

Ultimately, the Team Leader is the foundation on which the future of the financial team rests (see the pyramid below). Every one of the 15 performance factors comprising the 21st Century Financial Team Model requires "hands-on" leadership—at least in the first three stages of development.

During the initial phases of team development, the most costly mistake leaders make is taking the "hands-off" approach. Because many leaders regard themselves as financial professionals first, and leaders/managers second (if not third or fourth), they often treat their teams like old-fashioned wind-up toys. They want to turn a key and watch them go. Too often, your team *will* go, but straight into a brick wall. The lesson is that the four-stage development process requires careful planning and takes time and effort. It can't be artificially rushed, and skipping the *Forming Checklist*, regardless of how painful the exercise might appear, is a mistake. Once a team is properly formed, you must still keep a steady hand on the helm to prevent the group from tearing apart into squabbling cliques, especially during the *Storming Stage*. The following are three of the 15 specific ***performance factors*** directly associated with effective Team Leaders:

Performance Factor #1—Leads and inspires. A team's overall performance or lack thereof, is ultimately the responsibility of the Team Leader. An effective leader leads by example. He or she is the team's primary Rainmaker, and inspires other members to higher levels of performance. Not a team meeting goes by where Rainmaking, pipeline tracking and specific prospecting action steps aren't discussed.

Let me introduce you to Jack. Not only is he an effective Team Leader, he is mentoring one of his junior partners in the art of Rainmaking. Whenever he and his protégé are out-of-office prospecting, they always communicate their whereabouts to the other team members and involve them in assisting with the follow-up actions. These range from scheduling a call or meeting and sending a follow-up email or note, to assembling a financial organizer or financial plan, to having a "surprise and delight" gift delivered.

Much of this can be attributed to a personal commitment to excellence in every aspect of the team's performance. This was not simply a team sound-bite: Jack operates under the philosophy that you communicate clearly, treat people properly, and you should inspect what you expect. In addition to weekly team meetings (always conducted from a written agenda), the team holds half-day quarterly reviews that are held off-site, and a two-day annual retreat that is also off-site. It is during these retreats that team camaraderie is reinforced, and everyone works to make certain they contribute to the team's ongoing growth and development.

Performance Factor #2—Solves Problems and Corrects Mistakes. Good Team Leaders exercise good judgment. This does not mean that elite teams are free of problems. Murphy's Law still surfaces from time to time. The difference with Jack's team is twofold: 1) team members have been given authority to solve every client problem possible and correct any mistake they encounter; and 2) every solved problem and corrected mistake is documented, and Jack solves all large problems and corrects any major mistakes that require his judgment and oversight. The above is consistent with all elite teams, because no problem or mistake lingers or is swept under the rug. Hence, these teams present the outward appearance of being problem-free.

Performance Factor #3—Oversees the Team's Compensation Agreement. Within the best teams, compensation is clear and fair, so members don't quarrel over money. Jack uses his quarterly off-sites to bonus his support personnel if the team is hitting its metrics and contributing as he expects. Because his team is usually experiencing growth and achieving quarterly benchmarks, Jack's challenge is to make certain that everyone understands that each bonus check is earned. Like every good Team Leader, he recognizes that it's very easy for support personnel (as salaried employees) to regard their bonus as a standard part of their compensation package. Compensation issues tend to surface whenever the current bonus check is smaller than the previous one. Jack takes great pains to ensure that each individual understands the connection between performance and the bonus check. Partners are rewarded in terms of partnership shares at the two-day annual retreat.

It's obvious that Jack is very involved in leading his team. This is work. It requires hands-on involvement. Many senior advisors (soon to be Team Leaders) are much too casual during the Forming stage of team development and, therefore, completely unprepared to become immersed in the performance factors we have benchmarked to effective Team Leadership. Jack's attention to these performance factors has enabled his team to accelerate its journey through Tuckman's stages of development.

Only when a team reaches the Performing stage can leaders loosen the reins and delegate more freely. In a sense, they simply coordinate the teams' efforts as they move forward. And with dedicated leadership, the team *will* move forward. But at no time is there a place for casual leadership.

Jack embraced each of these performance factors, so it's no coincidence that he is the leader of an extremely successful financial team. They far exceeded the results benchmarked from our study by bringing in $83 million in new assets the previous year, and they were on track to exceed that high-water mark when I met with them. Not only was Jack the primary Rainmaker, leading by example, he had taken the time and invested the energy over the past three years to mentor a junior advisor in the fine art of Rainmaking.

Everyone was accountable for performing her role to the highest level of excellence. In addition, Jack made certain that each team member was responsible for personal development in specific areas. For example, one partner was in the process of getting his Certified Financial Planner designation, another was studying alternative investments, and his practice manager was taking a course in Microsoft Excel. Of course, one partner was learning how to become a Rainmaker.

Leadership is the foundation of every team. Without effective leadership there is no chance that the other performance factors will operate. Without effective leadership results are rarely sustained. It should come as no surprise, therefore, that Jack's team had all 15 performance factors in operation.

Because history is my avocation (I'm always reading biographies of famous people), I'm a firm believer that we can learn valuable lessons from history, especially on the topic of leadership. To that end, I have included a number of side-bar examples that can serve as both a training ground and inspiration to a Team Leader.

Using Dr. Tuckman's team development model, the "Black Book" sidebar illustrates how General George Marshall's years of careful planning enabled him to form a leadership team that would eventually defeat Nazi Germany. There was nothing casual about the names that went into his *Black Book*, and there was never a lack of oversight and hands-on involvement in his leading Ike, his chosen field leader.

Leadership Lesson: The Little Black Book

Well before the United States entered World War II, George Marshall—who was Army Chief of Staff during the conflict—realized that World War I had settled nothing. He predicted that the Treaty of Versailles was merely an interlude in a European Civil War that would once again spread worldwide.

Marshall was certain that the next global conflict "would be so bloody and horrible that its breadth would dwarf anything that had happened before. He knew that he would play a central role in this conflict, so he began to write the names of officers he respected in a little black book that he kept with him at all times. When he was finally placed in a position to build the army that would defend his nation, he referred to the names in his book and chose the generals he thought would be his nation's greatest commanders." Among the names in his little black book were Dwight Eisenhower, George Patton and Omar Bradley.[1]

Marshall's little black book highlights the first, and most important step, any leader must take when forming a financial team: getting "the right people on the bus" (to quote author Jim Collins).

But Marshall didn't choose the names in his book by merely assessing the technical, tactical or strategic competencies of the

[1] Perry, Mark. *Partners in Command: George Marshall and Dwight Eisenhower in War and Peace.* New York: The Penguin Press, 2007, pg. 4.

officers he encountered between the wars. The man who eventually became Marshall's trusted "second in command"—Dwight Eisenhower—was selected for that role as much because he shared the older man's worldview and unwavering optimism as for his administrative talents and tireless efforts to hold together the "stormy" coalition of British and American forces. In other words, Marshall chose Ike because he was committed to the same vision of how to conduct the war, and then how to maintain the peace.

Furthermore, once Ike's relationship with Marshall settled into the *Performing Stage* (and it didn't take long) the Chief of Staff allowed his junior almost complete freedom to make decisions. In fact, Marshall almost never second-guessed Eisenhower's actions, whether those actions concerned how/where to launch the next invasion of Nazi-occupied North Africa or Europe or whether/how to relieve an overly cautious (or insubordinate) general of command.

The Eisenhower and Patton sidebar illustrates another mark of a true Team Leader. Performance was always the objective, and as long as there was work to be done, it was essential to keep the right people on the bus. The lesson for every Team Leader is simple: as long as your team is focused on performance (growth), high-maintenance but talented team members can be tolerated. Why? Because the trouble they stir up is usually minor compared to the results they are delivering. However, whenever performance slows, which means the high-maintenance team member has more time on his hands, the trouble he causes is no longer a minor event. If unchecked, it will keep a team from regaining performance momentum, and probably land the team back in the *Storming* stage.

Leadership Lesson: Patton Gets Off the Bus

The last situation occurred on many occasions, but it happened most famously a few months after VE Day in 1945—when Eisenhower fired General Patton.

If you've ever watched George C. Scott's Oscar-winning performance as Patton in the 1970 movie of that name, you know that Patton wasn't the most "politically correct" of American generals. In fact, he was a swaggering, hard-driving man convinced of his

God-given destiny to achieve victory over the Germans. But he was also a brilliant tank commander. And what most moviegoers don't know is that he and Eisenhower had been very good friends since the early 1920s, when they developed some revolutionary ideas of how tanks should be used on future battlefields.

Eisenhower stuck with Patton, despite a number of incidents that caused a firestorm in the media, including the slapping and manhandling of at least three GIs who were suffering from Post Traumatic Stress Syndrome, a condition (poorly understood at the time) that Patton considered a coward's ticket home.

Eisenhower kept Patton "on the bus" because he knew that he was possibly the only general with the skills, daring and tenacity to race across France to Berlin. But once that was accomplished, Patton's flaws came to outweigh his talents. When Patton publicly criticized de-Nazification, saying America needed the Germans to mount an attack on the Russians, compared "this Nazi thing" to a "Democratic and Republican election fight," and made anti-Semitic statements in the immediate wake of the Holocaust, Eisenhower didn't hesitate to fire him.

You might be thinking, "Why all the historical emphasis on leadership? I get it." Well, fair comment, but as our politicians in Washington and corporate executives on Wall Street have demonstrated, "getting it" and judiciously using it is not always the same thing. It's become very obvious that leadership is a rare commodity. It is much more than a snazzy sound-bite. Teams are starved for effective leadership, as are affluent investors. There is no doubt about it: well-led financial teams are the future.

Let this be a reminder that the *Forming, Storming, Norming* and *Performing* model of team development is not always a one-way street to eventual AND PERMANENT success. It's not uncommon for some teams to endlessly see-saw between all four stages, depending on changes in circumstances, personnel and the attitudes of team members. Teams evolve and devolve. Teams have life-spans (though they can be continuously reformed without completely destroying the original foundations).

So, while leaders can loosen the reins and delegate more freely, becoming more "hands-off" during the Performing stage, this state of affairs is never permanent! The leader must keep his finger on the pulse of the team's health, monitor its evolution (or devolution), and quickly adopt a more "hands-on" approach when necessary. Most important, she must be ready to bring "new passengers" on the bus, and kick off anyone who isn't performing up to expectations.

Team Leaders can also change. Chuck, our Foundations Team Leader, underwent a radical transformation.

From Hands-Off to Hats Off!

Chuck was a hands-off leader. Because of his talent for managing money and growing his practice to $2 million in production and $300 million in assets, he allowed his ego to grow to the extent that it interfered with the core of who he really was. He liked adulation.

Knowing that he needed to create a team if he wanted to continue to grow without burning himself out (he was always fairly self-aware), he formed a team in precisely the wrong way. To use Jim Collins' language, Chuck got the "wrong people on the bus" when he hired two junior advisors and the very attractive and completely under-qualified Sally as administrative assistant.

From there, Chuck allowed his junior advisors to play him like a fiddle by massaging his ego, getting the team more recognition in the firm, having a video made for the firm, and giving Chuck a false sense of confidence that these two studs had everything under control. In fact, Chuck could even work from home if he liked. Which he frequently did, even allowing the junior advisors to run his weekly team meeting (he'd dial in from home).

He basically delegated all marketing (Rainmaking) to his junior advisors, delegated the practice management) to Sally (who was under the thumb of the junior advisors) and let the junior advisors take "pot-shots" at Ben.

Once Chuck realized that he'd been duped by these "young Turks," he quickly admitted that it was all his fault. He recognized one simple fact: he could not delegate Team Leadership.

He also learned that as a Team Leader, you inspect what you expect—you place accountability procedures in place to keep everyone both honest and accountable.

He recognized that he *had* to become the primary Rainmaker. And with some simple coaching from yours truly, he became a master in short order. He joined a country club (he was a good golfer who never had time to play) and began the process of schmoozing with strategic intent. He also learned how to keep his antenna out, source affluent prospects within his client's centers-of-influence and to orchestrate personal introductions. He personally ran every team meeting, and he did background checks on all new team members from then on.

The best Team Leaders recognize that change is inevitable, and are prepared to effectively respond. In some cases, this requires the Team Leader to change his style of leadership, management, communication, delegation, etc. and/or even guide the team back through the *Forming, Storming* and *Norming* phases—guide in a *controlled fashion,* that is.

In addition to history, I also love business, sports and politics. In the upcoming sidebars, you will notice examples of some very public leaders, who (like Chuck) also changed.

Because leadership is so intertwined with judgment, it can be a very fragile commodity. However, a negative can quickly be turned into a positive. On the flip-side, leaders are always one judgment call away from being questioned about their abilities. Growing up in White Plains, New York, I was a NFL Giants' fan before many of their current competitors existed. Needless to say, I've followed their ups and downs closely, and it dawned on me that their 2008 Super Bowl victory offers a wonderful, but not so obvious, lesson in leadership. I've attempted to outline the lesson in the sidebar without too much bias.

Leadership Lesson:
New York Giants Coach Tom Coughlin

Coughlin was fired as head coach of the NFL Jacksonville Jaguars. Although he had a good team, he was considered too intense, too tough on players, and much too distant—an unapproachable taskmaster in the mold of Bill Parcells (his mentor). His first couple of seasons as head coach with the Giants were no different, and his players were rebelling, (much as they did in Jacksonville, but New York is a much bigger stage). Two star players, Tikki Barber and

Jeromey Shockey, spoke out publicly regarding the negative atmosphere created by his coaching style.

For a myriad of reasons, the Giants, under Coughlin's leadership, seemed never to reach the Performing stage of team development. They seemed to be locked in the *Storming-Norming* trap.

This finally caused ownership to meet with Coughlin during the 2007 off-season to express their concerns. The result of ownership's intervention was that Coughlin made a commitment to change his personal coaching style. He formed a players committee to meet with him weekly to discuss issues. He created a new open-door policy, and made a serious effort to listen to what his players were saying. He remained a tough coach, but also listened to his wife, who advised that he let the players experience the same man that his family had experienced—a caring husband and father. He did. And the Giants defied all odds to win the 2008 Super Bowl.

It might be a coincidence, but neither Barber nor Shockey were playing (Barber retired and Shockey was on the disabled list). The Giants still had to work through all four stages of team development, but they avoided the *Storming-Norming* trap and kept their focus on the highest levels of performance. That's solid leadership!

Another Leadership Lesson from History

After World War II, Harry Truman said that the Allies were very lucky to have won that war. In my view, luck had less to do with it than the leadership qualities of the people that George Marshall brought together to fight Germany and Japan. Throughout the war, rivalries between the Army, Navy and Army Air Corps (later the Air Force), between individual commanders within the U.S. military and between commanders serving in the American, British and French militaries, often threatened to wreck the Allied war effort. It was only because of the leadership of men like FDR, Marshall, Eisenhower and others that the team managed to operate more often in the *Norming* and *Performing* Stages than the *Storming* Stage.

Sadly, too few people are students of history. For instance, most Americans know the Allies won World War II, but few can identify the leaders aside from Churchill, FDR, Eisenhower and Patton. And very few are aware of the leadership challenges that were overcome. The simple fact that an American General, Eisenhower, was given supreme command, created resentment among many of the British (and some American) brass, who thought they were passed over—particularly the talented, ego-centric General Bernard Law Montgomery. The fact that General Eisenhower was able recover from numerous backslides into the *Storming-Norming* trap is a lesson for every Team Leader.

Horizontal Teams

Who leads in a team of equals? That's a great question that rarely finds an easy answer. This is one of the reasons why so many financial teams of equal partnerships fail to reach their potential. They are not effectively led. Co-leadership, whether it's two, three, or four partners (choose your number) is never effective. Could you imagine if Eisenhower, Patton, and Montgomery were all co-leaders of the Allied forces?

In a team of equals, which is how we define a horizontal team, someone has to step-up and take the lead. On the rare occasion, one partner has the natural take-charge attributes and the other partners are glad to acquiesce. However, this is the exception not the rule. The norm is that an equal partner does not want a boss. Which highlights a major misconception amongst partners in horizontal financial teams; the team leader is not the boss of the other partners. The team leader is the partner who has accepted the responsibility to inspire and oversee the team along its critical path to their long-range goals (business plan).

What I have seen work effectively in these teams of equals is what I refer to as an annual Team Leader rotation. It's almost like one partner becomes the managing director for the year. This annual role requires a slightly greater commitment and there should be a small annual stipend attached because of the additional time involved. The secret is that each partner must share the team vision and be completely committed to the team's business plan and annual metrics scorecard.

This annual role will require more hands-on involvement such as working more closely with the Practice Manager and helping organize and creating the agenda for the weekly team meetings. It will also require personal involvement in individual performance reviews, performance up-dates for quarterly off-sites, and overseeing the planning of the team's annual retreat. Think of assuming annual responsibility for being the last line for major decision making and problem solving. But for horizontal teams to be effective in this type of revolving leadership, each partner has to pitch-in whenever necessary. The partner in rotation is not an island as no partner can ever be completely free of leadership responsibilities.

Lessons for Team Leaders

Highly effective leadership is a rare commodity. One reason is that it requires hands-on, experiential learning. In other words, you have to learn from your own mistakes. Yes, I know. I lectured you about becoming students of history, but the most effective Team Leaders master their craft by rolling-up their sleeves and leading teams. They make mistakes, they learn from their mistakes, they learn how to blend different personalities, they learn how to delegate, how to empower others, and they learn how to exercise good judgment. None of this can be fully learned in a classroom or from a book.

Summary

- A team in the first three stages of development requires the "hands-on" management of the Team Leader.
- Leaders of Elite Financial Teams incorporate these key ***Performance Factors*** into their role: 1) leading performance, 2) solving problems and correcting mistakes, and 3) overseeing the team compensation agreement.
- The *Forming, Storming, Norming* and *Performing* model of team development is not always a one-way street to permanent success. It's not uncommon for some teams to endlessly see-saw between all four stages.

- The best leaders recognize that change is inevitable, and are prepared to respond to changes. Sometimes, this requires the leader to change his/her own style of leadership and/or guide the team back through the *Forming, Storming* and *Norming* phases.
- Leadership is a skill that must be nurtured and developed. It requires experiential learning.
- There are many leadership lessons that can be learned from studying historical leaders.
- Effective Team Leaders get the right people on the team.
- Horizontal teams need effective leadership.
- Effective Team Leadership is a MUST for sustaining high levels of performance.

4

The Business Development Process

(Performance Factors 4, 5 & 6)

> *26.2% of teams report having a long-range business plan that's effectively linked to business development activities.*
>
> —Factoid, Financial Team Research

Charles Kettering, the great inventor and industrialist, once said, "My interest is in the future because I'm going to spend the rest of my life there." This is a sobering thought that effective Team Leaders take seriously. They understand that Kettering's statement raises an important question: Is the team's future going to be shaped by circumstances, or will we "raise our game" and take steps to become an elite team?

Let's take a look at the three *Performance Factors* (4, 5 & 6) that our research found consistently within the Business Development Process of elite teams.

Performance Factor #4: Business Planning

Our research on financial teams reveals that teams in the elite stage:

- Have a long-range business plan that covers two years or more.
- Consistently link the execution of all business development strategies and activities to the team's long-range business plan.

The continual growth of a team, based on metrics such as acquiring new affluent clients, increasing production and bringing in new assets, usually requires a plan. Spontaneous growth rarely occurs. An elite team's business development process is anchored by its business plan. This serves as a road map, guiding the team into the future.

Elite Financial Teams take their business plans very seriously. They recognize that in order to implement the long-range plan, it must be linked directly to business development strategies and activities. Our research indicates that developing such a plan contributes significantly to a highly rewarding team experience.

The opposite is true whenever the link to business development was missing. For example, The Founder's Group (whose story we've been following) drafted a first-rate business plan, but there was no direct link to business development, so no critical path was established, which made it much easier to ignore. And ignore it they did.

In order to move the team forward, this business plan must be:

Real. Too many business plans are merely intellectual exercises. They look pretty on paper, but have more in common with an MBA thesis that presents a "perfect" plan than a realistic blueprint. The acid test for a real plan is simple: can you distill it onto the back of a business envelope?

You'd be surprised, or maybe you wouldn't, at the initial reaction I get when conducting what I refer to as *The Back-of-the-Envelope Drill* during our workshops. The first reaction is usually disbelief. It's as though participants haven't completely understood the instructions. "He can't seriously be suggesting that I distill our business plan to the back of an envelope." Once it dawns on everyone that I'm dead serious, a few get busy while the majority sits silently, with dumbfounded expressions on their faces. The problem of this perplexed majority is that they have never connected their business plans to the day-to-day realities of growing their enterprises.

Minus this connection, it becomes obvious to the Team Leaders in my workshops that their business plans are not really functioning tools.

Measurable. What are the specifics? How many new affluent clients will be acquired by the team? What is the projected net new asset target? What is the overall production or revenue target? What percentage of revenue is targeted as fee-based versus commission-based? How many smaller clients does the team need to "shed"? How many clients will receive help organizing all of their financial documents in a Financial Organizer?

Time Sensitive. The long-range business plan may project three to five years into the future, but your annual targets must be time sensitive. At The Oechsli Institute, we recommend a one-year metrics system. (Basically, the one-year metrics system consists of annual goals linked to the long-range plan. In other words, if you're not close to your time-sensitive annual targets, you're not likely to reach your long-range goals.) The one- year system is further segmented into Quarterly Metrics—essentially a quarterly review system designed to strengthen the time sensitivity of the annual goals.

Clear to Every Team Member. Clarity should include the big picture, long-range business plan, the annual and quarterly metrics (goals), individual roles and responsibilities linked to the metrics, and future growth opportunities that will result from achieving the long-range plan. It's important that even support personnel understand how they are contributing to the overall success of the team. I always recommend a bonus pool that speaks to this issue, where everyone who contributes, at whatever level, receives a share of the bonus pool. This requires hands-on leadership!

The absence of a long-range business plan often suggests that, rather than a team in the true sense of the word, you have a group of individuals who simply share some resources while focusing on their own businesses. If you don't have a team business plan, you need to ask: "Do we really want to become an Elite Financial Team?" If you answer YES, you are ready to follow the outline below:

1. Meet as a team to create a team business plan that covers at least two years or more. You will want to ensure that each team member's personal goals are aligned to the team's business plan. It's important that everyone pulls together.

2. Once your team's business plan is in place, and individual goals are aligned with it, define the connection between the team plan and each member's weekly and daily business development activities. At this stage, identify any activities that are not adequately linked to your team's business plan. Any activity that has no relationship to the long-range business plan should be eliminated.
3. Finally, thoroughly review your team's plan so you can say, "Our team has a long-range business plan covering two years or more, and we consistently link all of our business development strategies and activities to the plan."

Once you have your business plan up and running, you'll want to review it periodically to ensure that it remains linked to your annual goals. The most natural time to do this is during performance reviews. Quarterly off-sites are a perfect forum, but many elite teams review performance on a monthly basis. Either way, there are never any surprises that have been unaddressed for more than three months. If you have the good fortune to discover that you are exceeding your team's annual goal projections, you can adjust your long-range business plan accordingly. On the other hand, if you have fallen behind your team's annual goal projections, it is important to determine why and make the necessary adjustments. You can always correct a sub-par three months, but it's extremely difficult to make up a bad year.

The following vignette illustrates the complexity of a functional team, but also how a business plan works as a strong antidote to these five dysfunctions.

The Five Dysfunctions of a Team

In his book with the above title, author and management consultant Patrick Lencioni writes:

"Genuine teamwork in most organizations remains as elusive as it has ever been . . . . Organizations fail to achieve teamwork because they unknowingly fall prey to five natural but dangerous pitfalls, which I call the five dysfunctions.

These dysfunctions can be mistakenly interpreted as five distinct issues that can be addressed in isolation, but in reality they form an interrelated model, making susceptibility to even one of them potentially lethal for the success of a team . . . .

1. The first dysfunction is an **absence of trust** among team members. Essentially, this stems from their unwillingness to be vulnerable within the group. Team members who are not genuinely open with one another about their mistakes and weaknesses make it impossible to build a foundation of trust.
2. This failure to build trust is damaging because it sets the tone for the second dysfunction: **fear of conflict**. Teams that lack trust are incapable of engaging in unfiltered and passionate debate of ideas. Instead, they resort to veiled discussions and guarded comments.
3. A lack of healthy conflict is a problem because it ensures the third dysfunction of a team: **lack of commitment**. Without having aired their opinions in the course of passionate and open debate, team members rarely, if ever, buy in and commit to decisions, though they may feign agreement during meetings.
4. Because of this lack of real commitment and buy-in, team members develop an **avoidance of accountability**, the fourth dysfunction. Without committing to a clear plan of action, even the most focused and driven people often hesitate to call their peers on actions and behaviors that seem counterproductive to the good of the team.
5. Failure to hold one another accountable creates an environment where the fifth dysfunction can thrive. **Inattention to results** occurs when team members put their individual needs (such as ego, career development, or recognition) or even the needs of their divisions above the collective goals of the team.

And so, like a chain with just one link broken, teamwork deteriorates if even a single dysfunction is allowed to flourish.

Another way to understand this model is to take the opposite approach—a positive one—and imagine how members of a truly cohesive team behave:

1. "They trust one another.
2. "They engage in unfiltered conflict around ideas.
3. "They commit to decisions and plans of action.
4. "They hold one another accountable for delivering against those plans.
5. "They focus on the achievement of collective results."[2]

Throughout these chapters you will find exercises to help leaders and team members overcome these dysfunctions, and other problems.

Performance Factor #5: Upgrading Existing Clients

Elite teams position themselves to be the "go-to" financial coordinator of all their clients' assets. Therefore, whenever an existing client isn't receiving the full menu of services, these teams exercise a repositioning strategy to fully upgrade the client. This is different than periodically contacting the client and asking for additional assets or pitching another service. Top teams strive to fully monetize each client relationship by working constantly at being the "go-to" financial coordinator.

If a client has assets elsewhere, your objective is to reposition your team with this person. This can be done by:

- Scheduling a meeting to explain that your team is capable of coordinating every aspect of the family's financial affairs. It is essential, of course, that you *actually possess* the capabilities you are communicating.
- Promise to organize and coordinate all of their financial documents. I recommend presenting them with some type of organizational tool that can serve as tangible evidence of this process.

---

[2] Lencioni, Patrick. *The Five Dysfunctions of a Team: A Leadership Parable.* San Francisco: Jossey-Bass, 2002, pp-187-190.

- Explain how your quarterly and annual reviews are scheduled, and how this benefits them.
- Talk about the outside experts you might use (if you use them): estate-planning attorneys, CPAs, and so on.

Done properly, this upgrade process can be viewed as a triple win: (1) every client gets high-level consistent experiences, (2) all team members are engaged in the client experience, and (3) your team fully monetizes each client relationship.

Performance Factor #6: Attracting New Clients

The best teams are characterized by two important factors regarding new affluent client acquisition (Rainmaking):

1. The Team Leader or another designated senior partner takes primary responsibility for new client acquisition.
2. On average, these acquisition efforts bring in 10 or more $1 million or greater relationships per year. This means the team member responsible for new client acquisition has achieved Rainmaker status. Whenever there is more than one senior partner, each partner should be responsible for 10 or more new relationships a year.

If your team is not acquiring affluent clients as above, it's not functioning as a true financial team. Teams in the elite stage take Rainmaking very seriously. Therefore, I suggest you consider:

- Reconfirming the affluent client acquisition role, associated responsibilities and marketing activities. Each partner should share, to some degree, in this area. There are several methods by which teams can divide up their "marketing department." For some industry perspective, take a look at the following data from our 2007—2009 Financial Team research:

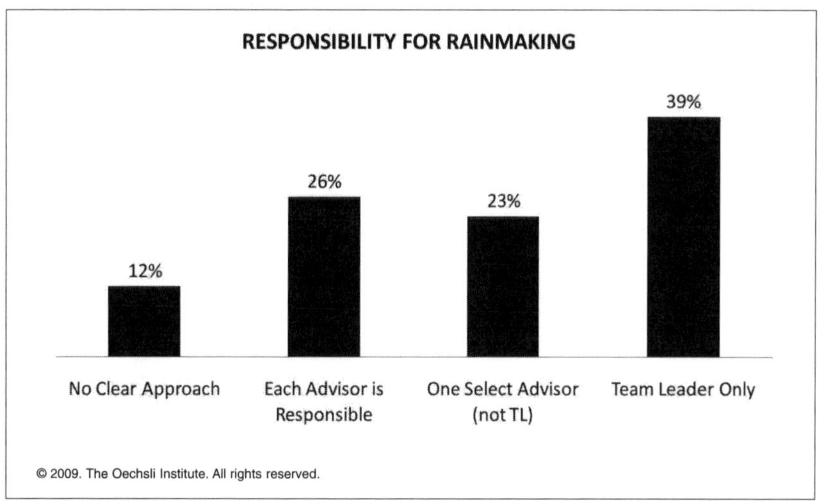

- Determining whether the team member(s) responsible for acquiring new affluent clients know *which* marketing activities to engage in and *how* to perform these activities. Our research on the affluent tells us, these activities had better focus on word-of-mouth influence and penetrating centers-of-influence. 65% consulted their friends, family, colleagues or another professional when searching for a new professional.

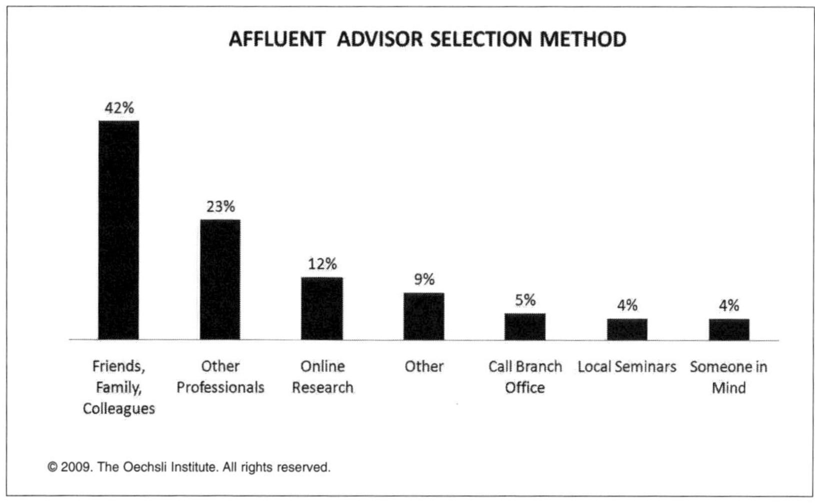

- Agreeing on the target market—the ideal affluent client. Here's another graph from our Team research. We asked, "On what level of client does your team focus its marketing efforts?"

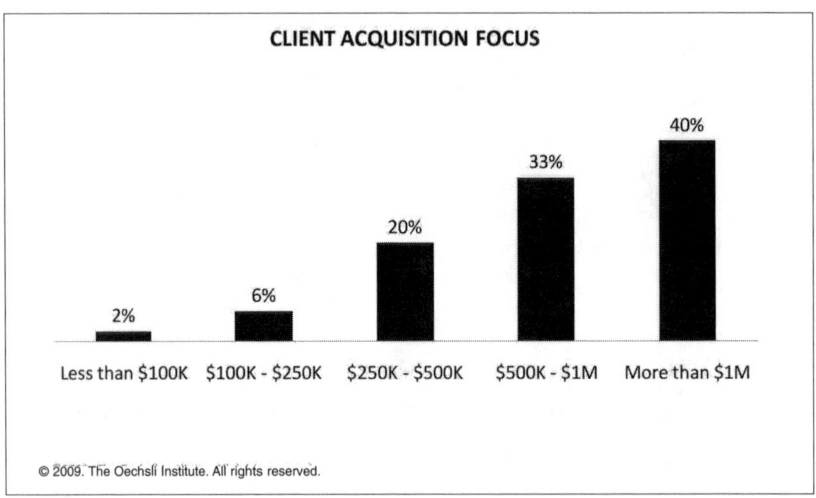

- Developing a specific action plan for the team member responsible—sourcing one affluent prospect name each day from a center-of-influence, getting introduced to an affluent prospect, networking in affluent social circles, penetrating affluent centers-of-influence, spending time with strategic alliance partners (CPAs, estate-planning attorneys, etc.).
- Activating accountability for executing the above action plan.

Affluent client acquisition is a critical component of every Elite Financial Team. It also is the Achilles heel of many teams that never reach elite status. That's because it requires sales skills that are so refined, so well honed, that they are seamless. When these skills are lacking, affluent client acquisition becomes extremely uncomfortable, which is why many Team Leaders develop avoidance patterns.

Not long ago, I was asked to salvage a team consisting of three senior partners, all of equal stature, in their New Mexico offices. Although they referred to themselves as DBW Financial Team, there was no Team Leader, no business plan and no team goals. Each financial advisor served his own clients, and each handled them his own way—in other words, there was no consistent client experience or process across the team. Earlier, they had verbally agreed to transition their clients into a particular fee-based platform, but only one partner was doing so, and doing so at a *very* slow pace. This was not an issue at first, because there was no accountability, and no one was actively engaged in Rainmaking activities.

One of the partners attempted to become a Rainmaker, but after a half-hearted month-long effort, he gave up. In his mind, it made no sense to "bust his butt" if his partners weren't going to help acquire affluent clients. All of this created tension that the "team members" tried to mitigate by bringing a junior advisor onboard.

Her alleged role was to help manage smaller clients (they had over 900 total households) and engage in marketing activities. Because she was a go-getter, and actively performed key Rainmaking activities, the partners hoped she would assume this role for them. They fed her some assets of smaller clients as a token of good faith, her manager signed-off, and for six months, she was the newest member of a very dysfunctional team.

She realized her plight after three months. The partners were simply exploiting her. She didn't really need them. They needed *her* Rainmaking skills. When she left soon thereafter, the team found itself *Storming*. They argued about Rainmaking, about losing their top-performing junior advisor, about their work ethics, about compensation, etc. Needless to say, my involvement was a day late and a dollar short. The "team" suffered a performance-damaging divorce. Today, they are once again three separate, average-level producers whose client acquisition efforts rest on a plateau of mediocrity.

Walter in Chicago was the founder of another three-person team. Each team member had known the others for years, they respected one another, and went through a serious courtship (one advisor had to switch firms to join the team). Because of Walter's military experience (he was a former officer), he assumed command of the team.

At first, everything moved ahead very well. They progressed to the *Norming* stage, their practice management was improving, but accountability was always suspect, which meant their business plan was not a working document. Because it wasn't linked to their business development efforts, there was no way to measure performance.

Each advisor was a decent producer, but nobody complained until Walter began taking more time off than his partners. He took a two-week vacation that wasn't scheduled. (Curiously, they had overlooked vacations in their business plan.) Everything came to a head when Walter's wife gave birth to their first child. Walter stayed home with her for two weeks, claiming he was working from home. As one of his partners told me, "I thought his *wife* had the baby!" Quickly, the other partners got annoyed, but took Walter at his word that he was prospecting from home—that he was doing his Rainmaking activities.

Unfortunately (or fortunately), the proof is in the results. Walter was not bringing in any new business, and when he finally returned to the office, he was leaving early to "go on Rainmaking appointments." This group soon went through an ugly divorce. These former friends no longer talk to each other, and that's after spending more than a year pre-planning their team launch!

Neither of these divorced teams was capable of sustaining any type of consistent Rainmaking activity, much less results. There was a lack of accountability associated to their business plans, and quite frankly, a lack of know-how. Thanks to this, neither team linked the senior partners to specific rainmaking activities. In addition, neither team had an effective leader, as the senior partners were not leading by example. Instead of solving problems for affluent clients and strengthening loyalty, they were creating problems for themselves. There was simply no senior partner accountability connected to their business plans.

As I mentioned at the top of this chapter, Founder's Group Team Leader, Chuck, developed a first-rate business plan. Unfortunately, Chuck's plan was an academic exercise, because he never exercised the leadership to make it a working document. He liked the idea of showing it to other Team Leaders at his firm's big-producer functions, and the plan never failed to impress everyone. This, of course, fed Chuck's ego, especially since nobody asked how closely he was following the plan, how he was measuring the performance of team members, etc.

Chuck's plan was pure fiction—a fantasy that eventually caused his team to re-visit the *Storming* stage and break apart. To his credit, Chuck was undeterred. He learned his lessons well, and has since developed an elite team. However, these lessons were painful, and he had to work extremely hard at becoming a true leader.

Summary

- Every Elite Financial Team must implement a long-range business plan linked to its business development strategies and activities.
- Three *Performance Factors* are consistent in all top teams: business planning, upgrading existing clients, and attracting new affluent clients.
- This plan must be REAL, MEASURABLE, TIME SENSITIVE AND CLEAR TO EVERY TEAM MEMBER.
- The Business Plans of Elite Financial Teams incorporate solving problems with FedEx-level efficiency and first-rate customer service.
- A poorly prepared business plan, or a good one that isn't followed, isn't worth the paper it's printed on.
- You should be able to transfer the "guts" of your team's business plan to the back of an envelope.
- Effective Team Leaders are students of the affluent and their understanding permeates throughout the team.
- Elite Financial Teams are not problem free, they solve problems.
- The affluent select financial professionals based on word-of-mouth influence.
- Team Leader accountability must be directly connected to the team's business plan.

5

The Client Loyalty Process

(Performance Factors 7 & 8)

> *19.2% of teams did not lose any clients last year for reasons outside of death or other factors totally outside their control.*
>
> —Factoid, Financial Team Research

The early 21st century is among the best of times for affluent Americans, but the recent meltdown within the financial world has transformed all of this into ancient history. Today's top 20% of U.S. income earners are perpetually fearful of falling into a financial abyss. They want someone, some entity, to protect them from themselves and Wall Street, which is why every elite team makes a point of truly understanding the needs, wants and quirks of today's affluent consumer. It is from this vantage point that they align their services. *Important Note:* the affluent expect you to deliver everything they want—and then some—in good *and* bad markets. And never before has the trust factor weighed so heavily on individual advisors and teams.

FedEx Efficiency Benchmarks

Recently, I forgot to bring my BlackBerry power cord with me after departing on a four-day lecture trip. I had my assistant send the cord by overnight delivery—but I forgot to specify FedEx—to the Los Angeles hotel where I was staying for the first two days. I was originally scheduled to spend three nights, but was able to leave earlier, and failed to inform my assistant.

No harm, no foul. I had to leave by noon, and my package was guaranteed for delivery by noon. Unfortunately, this guarantee didn't translate into actual receipt. I informed the front desk and the concierge desk of my overnight package, the expected delivery time, my departure time and the urgency of the matter. They appeared eager to please, wrote down my name and the meeting room where I was speaking, and promised to deliver it. At 11:00 a.m., the meeting planners began checking on my package. No delivery—yet. They checked again at 11:15, 11:30 and 11:45 a.m.—no delivery. I checked at noon—no delivery. I even had the concierge desk use my tracking code, which indicated my package had arrived at LAX at 9:23 a.m.

They suggested I look in the alley beside the hotel to see if there was a delivery truck parked there. The only delivery vehicle was a FedEx truck, making its second drop of the morning.

My flight schedule was tight, so I was forced to leave without the power cord. As I was boarding the flight, my assistant called to inform me that USPS claimed to have delivered the package at 10:30 a.m., but they didn't know:

a. who signed for it;
b. why it wasn't delivered to me;
c. why nobody seemed to know it had arrived.

USPS blamed the hotel, and the hotel blamed USPS for not delivering the package to the concierge desk. In my view, blame-gaming is among the worst behaviors to engage in when a customer is not satisfied. Would some person step-up and just fix the problem!

Somehow, I knew that FedEx would have made certain I received my package. Their level of efficiency would have *guaranteed* that the package was signed for, they would know who signed for it, and they would know I had received it. You can be sure that these actions are linked to their business plan and they would never play the blame game. Part of it was my fault. In addition to forgetting my power cord and failing to tell my assistant of my schedule change, I also forgot to mention that we ALWAYS use FedEx when a delivery ABSOLUTELY must be made on time!

Elite Financial Teams execute! They follow through on promises, everyone takes ownership, and nobody plays the blame game. Accountability is the norm, and as a result, elite teams solve problems.

And because they are students of the affluent, Elite Financial Teams understand that the #1 Criterion for strengthening affluent loyalty is to solve a problem, communicate everything clearly, and make absolutely certain that the client understands, and agrees with, the proposed resolution. Obviously, this was a far cry from my power cord experience, and it is a serious challenge for any team that does not have a Practice Management Process that adheres to FedEx efficiency.

Leaders of Elite Financial Teams really understand the affluent. They recognize that they are an idiosyncratic species that requires constant attention to its needs, wants, biases and perceptions. This understanding permeates the team. It becomes part of the team's DNA.

Southwest Airlines Service Benchmarks

Southwest Airlines can board passengers faster than any other carrier I've flown, which is why they consistently outrank the competition in on-time flights. The entire crew pitches in to get passengers seated, luggage stored, and people out of the aisles. The PA system is used, pleasantly, to keep everyone moving to their seats so the aircraft can depart as scheduled. I've even seen pilots collecting trash, so there's no waiting around for the cleaning crew. On top of this, the hard-working employees have a great attitude, are passenger friendly, and give the appearance that they thoroughly enjoy their jobs. It's no coincidence that the company insists that its employees possess a sense of humor and a friendly disposition. Too bad this isn't a standard requirement for all jobs that involve serving the public.

As I was writing this chapter, I heard a story on National Public Radio. It just happened to be about customer satisfaction ratings regarding the airlines. It came as no surprise that the ratings of all the major carriers were low, but what caught my attention was that they had all dropped precipitously over the past three years, with my primary carrier (it has the most flights in and out of my home in Greensboro, NC), USAir, dead last. Anyone who flies is aware that the business model for the standard airline is broken—fuel costs, labor costs, etc. But with one element clearly within their control, customer service, all but one carrier has been getting worse.

You guessed it: according to the NPR segment, Southwest leads the pack, not only in customer satisfaction but in generating a profit. Go figure. Outside of learning how to run an airline from Southwest, that industry could learn a lot from Team Leaders of Elite Financial Teams. They know how to treat their clients.

Elite Financial Teams have a Southwest-style esprit des corps. Every team member, from the lowest-level support person to the senior partner, pitches in wherever necessary, and enjoys her role on the team. Everyone's degree of loyalty far surpasses anything else in the industry. You could make an argument that all of this should be part of a team's practice management or client loyalty process, and you wouldn't get an argument from me. They are inextricably linked. However, the teams that execute like FedEx and Southwest have incorporated this level of execution as part of their business plan.

Like Southwest Airlines, elite teams do not take this behavior for granted. Team Leaders set the tone, reinforce both positive attitudes and behavior, and ask someone to leave the team if they cannot live up to expectations.

Performance Factor #7: Affluent Client Retention

Performance Factor #8: Commitment to Excellence

Two critical *Performance Factors* (7 & 8) are consistent in the Client Loyalty Process of Elite Financial Teams: Affluent Client Retention and Commitment to Excellence. Why are these performance factors so critical to your team? Three reasons:

1. They are representative of every other aspect of your team's functionality.
4. You will never earn the loyalty of your affluent clients unless your team possesses a total commitment to excellence.
3. Because word-of-mouth influence is how the affluent make major purchase decisions, affluent client loyalty is the most statistically significant factor for affluent client acquisition.

Since the relationship between these two performance factors is inextricably linked, to each other and to affluent client acquisition, I'll discuss them together. It is from this interconnectivity that I was able to pinpoint the direct relationship between service, client loyalty and revenue, which I call the *service-loyalty-revenue nexus.* The following scenario tells the story.

While writing this chapter, I met with a financial team composed of three senior partners, two support staff and one intern. They managed over $300 million in assets, and though they had culled their clients, they still had too many: 200 of their households represented less than $10 million in assets. Topping the "to-do" list was Rainmaking, since the team had acquired only five new affluent relationships the previous year.

The partners had done their homework. Each had a list of potential prospects linked to an existing affluent client's center-of-influence. With a little Rainmaker coaching, they hoped, each partner could bring in 10 new affluent clients in the next 12 months. Their conservative calculations indicated that 30 new $1 million relationships, yielding $35 million in assets at 1%, would generate $350,000 in revenue. I liked their thinking and their creative math.

However, I soon discovered that this was not their only issue. The team had lost four good clients the previous year, thanks to serious gaps in their *service-loyalty-revenue nexus.* Not surprisingly, none of the partners had ever heard of this concept. Here's how I explained it to them.

High-level service combined with a comprehensive wealth management process develops loyal clients. Loyal clients directly impact revenue. Therefore, everything is inextricably linked (a nexus).

Using their simple math, I walked them through a cost-benefit ratio of $280,000 per client (details later), which meant the loss of four affluent clients translated into a hit of $1,120,000 to their projected revenue stream. Because none of the partners was a Rainmaker, the team had never assigned a concrete value to penetrating their top clients' centers-of-influence.

Let's back up, and start at the beginning of our *service-loyalty-revenue nexus.*

- **Service**

  Service and problem-solving are the most statistically significant criteria impacting affluent loyalty. When either is sub-par, dissatisfaction creeps into the relationship, and the cost is greater than most advisors realize.

- **Affluent Client Loyalty**

  As with team members, client loyalty must be earned over time. And this issue transcends client satisfaction, which is merely the minimum requirement.

Our research has identified 7 criteria that directly impact affluent loyalty:

- Resolving problems quickly and to my satisfaction.
- Meeting investment performance expectations.
- Clearly understanding my situation when giving advice.
- Notifying me of events that impact my portfolio.
- Caring about more than just my investments.
- Helping me create and execute a financial plan.
- The frequency of personal contact is meeting my needs.

Although these criteria appear to be common sense, from the perspective of the affluent, statistically significant gaps exist. Closing these gaps should be a fire-drill for every financial team. As you will discover, the cost/benefit ratio is dramatic.

- **Revenue (Cost-Benefit Ratio)**

  Loyal clients are your acre of diamonds if they:

  - Like you,
  - Trust you,
  - Respect you professionally relative to their current needs (wealth management process), and
  - Allow you to penetrate their centers-of-influence (COI).

As you know, word-of-mouth influence is the primary method the affluent use in making major purchase decisions, and determining who coordinates the family's financial affairs *is* a major decision. With that factoid in the equation, your existing affluent clients should be your primary source for new client acquisition.

Our research and experience tell us that each loyal affluent client should be capable of helping you acquire six similar clients from their centers-of-influence throughout the lifetime of your professional relationship.

Using these figures (six similar clients), let's take a closer look at the cost-benefit ratio that I shared with the partners above. To keep things simple, let's assume $1-million clients at a 1% fee.

Affluent Loyalty Cost-Benefit Ratio

Loyal Affluent Client	$1 million in investable assets
Annual Fee	1% ($10,000)
Loyalty Years	7 years
Total Revenue	$70,000

Assuming a total of six new affluent clients, adding one every 12 months (same $1 million profile) from your affluent client's centers-of-influence, consider the following over the same seven-year period.

Initial Affluent Client—7 years @ $10,000 a year =	$70,000
Year 2: one new affluent client—6 years @ $10,000 a year =	$60,000
Year 3: one new affluent client—5 years @ $10,000 a year =	$50,000
Year 4: one new affluent client—4 years @ $10,000 a year =	$40,000
Year 5: one new affluent client—3 years @ $10,000 a year =	$30,000
Year 6: one new affluent client—2 years @ $10,000 a year =	$20,000
Year 7: one new affluent client—1 year @ $10,000 a year =	$10,000
Affluent Client Cost-Benefit =	$280,000

Needless to say, these numbers ($280,000 x 4 lost clients = $1.12 million) got the attention of the partners. In fact, instead of trying to refute my math, they thought my numbers were low!

Many teams have a blind spot to this *service-loyalty-revenue nexus,* failing to recognize the value of exceeding the expectations of their best clients. Alas, this leaves them incapable of penetrating their centers-of-influence. The result is no growth, which leaves them somewhere in that *Storming-Norming trap.* An interesting side note: we have data indicating that only 19.9% of financial professionals have increased the amount of personal time spent with affluent clients during the subprime debacle that is in full gear as I write. This is a distinct opportunity for every Elite Financial Team.

A working understanding of this *service-loyalty-revenue nexus* is a powerful tonic for every team's client loyalty process. I am constantly amused by how simple concepts like this always separate the pros from the pretenders. Loyalty is personal; it requires your team to really know each affluent client.

A Middle-Class Mindset

One would think it common sense that in order to better attract, service and develop loyal affluent clients, financial service professionals would dedicate themselves to getting into their clients' minds, learning how they think and make decisions. However, common sense is not always common practice, and many financial teams still don't understand the affluent consumer they so desperately covet.

This understanding is critical in developing loyalty. Without developing strong loyalty among affluent clients, business development efforts will always be a struggle. As the service-loyalty-revenue nexus illustrates, it pays to understand what makes the affluent tick and act accordingly.

For instance, aside from the "super rich" (households with assets of more than $50 million), the majority of affluent Americans don't consider themselves rich. Taken at face value, this self-perception seems absurd. The typical top-quintile household has investable assets ranging from hundreds of thousands of dollars to tens of millions, owns vacation homes and luxury cars, sends the children to the best universities, and takes expensive vacations. But when you peel away the statistics and examine the mindsets, lifestyles and family backgrounds of the contemporary affluent, it makes perfect sense.

Financial Priorities of the Affluent
Oechsli Institute Research

1. Meet current living expenses and obligations.
2. Maintain current lifestyle in retirement.
3. Minimize taxes.
4. Protect against serious financial loss.
5. Organize and coordinate all financial documents.

Because elite teams understand today's affluent, they diligently avoid using the term "wealth" when marketing their services.

The top 5% of U.S. income earners enjoys an average pre-tax family income of $276,000 and pays 50% of all taxes. Little wonder, then, that our affluent surveys continually uncover affluent angst regarding taxes; our "Understanding the Affluent: America's Top Quintile Income Earners" discovered that the #3 Financial Priority of top quintile income earners is minimizing taxes!

As I wrote in *The Affluent Handbook*,[3] "Many of the wealthy have little in common with their millionaire forbears of the 19th and 20th centuries—and for good reason. Most do *not* trace their affluence to the "robber barons" of the Gilded Age, but to the prosperous middle class that emerged after World War II. In other words, their incomes, assets and lifestyles belie more humble roots—roots firmly planted in middle-class soil.

"About 93% of affluent Americans are self-made. They are CEOs, upper management, large and small business owners, self-employed professionals, partners in professional practices (doctors, CPAs, etc.), and successful high-commissioned salespeople. Although they tend to be hard chargers and consider themselves successful, as a rule they don't consider themselves "rich." Because of their drive and work ethic, however, they not only earn more money than most people, they have three times the amount of stress. Therefore, they don't like their precious time wasted, and they don't suffer fools.

As we have discussed, a team's current stage of development correlates directly to their client loyalty factor, or service-loyalty-revenue nexus. The more rapidly a team works through these stages of development, the more likely they are to provide the services, and offer the time and attention, that affluent clients demand.

> Demographically, the top-income households share many characteristics, one of the more notable being their origin in the decidedly middle class. . . . Today's affluent are living the American dream, with 90 percent coming from [the] middle-class. . . . [4]

"Whether you're a financial advisor, attorney or luxury retailer—you must understand that, when dealing with today's affluent American, you're usually dealing with someone who clings to a middle-class mindset. The typical affluent believes in working hard, saving and

---

[3] Oechsli, Matt. *The Affluent Handbook: Understanding America's Top Income Quintile.* [Overland Park Kansas: Wealth Management Press, 2008.]

[4] Danziger, Pamela N. *Let Them Eat Cake: Marketing Luxury to the Masses—as Well as the Classes*, Chicago: Dearborn Trade Publishing, 2005, p. 40.

investing, maintaining his current lifestyle, planning for retirement, and is not convinced that he's a member of America's elite."

An Age of Wisdom . . . and Skepticism

The affluent are looking for *unbiased* financial professionals—people they trust to guide them through the complexities of today's financial world. Most already have an accountant, but recognize that they need someone who can do more than compile yearly tax returns. Most have invested money in the stock market, but know they need more than advice on stock and bond purchases. Most own insurance policies, but recognize that they need someone who does more than sell insurance. They want someone to oversee the *entirety* of their family's financial affairs.

But affluent Americans are *very* discriminating. Your products and services had better be as advertised—and you'd better understand that YOU are the chief product—or prospective clients will hire your competitors. Advertising and marketing to this segment is tricky, and must be done with tact and finesse. Marketing campaigns must contain no false promises, yet be appealing enough to catch their attention. Wealthy clients shop for discounts, but discounting doesn't impact their loyalty. *Performance, service, and problem solving does!*

NOTHING is more important than making sure your clients are satisfied, not just at the moment of purchase but forever after. Too many sellers "drop the ball" once the customer has been "hooked," forgetting that a client's subsequent satisfaction will greatly impact his or her loyalty, including whether the person will steer influential friends, family and business associates your way. When deciding whether to use the same service provider again (another loyalty indicator), affluent respondents gave the strongest influence to:

- Any problems I encountered were resolved quickly and satisfactorily.
- They provided good service following my purchase.
- They previously provided information I needed to make a satisfactory decision.

Anatomy of a "Go-To Pro"

Since 1999, three different studies commissioned by The Oechsli Institute have revealed wide gaps between advisor performance and investor expectations.

Our latest study reveals what the wealthy want in their Primary Financial Coordinator. Survey respondents told us that this "go-to pro" must:

- Be proactive about contacting them when upcoming tax and other changes will impact their investment portfolio.
- Clearly reveal his/her fee structure.
- Clearly understand the client's goals and family situation when giving investment advice.
- Bring in experts to help with other financial areas.
- Help clients select the best asset mix for their investment portfolios.
- Help clients create formal financial plans.
- Help clients coordinate and organize all of their financial documents.
- Coordinate investment decisions.

It's no coincidence that our Elite Financial Teams give the affluent what they want . . . and then some. This engenders loyalty among team members (they feel proud of the service they're providing) and the clients. As simple as this might appear, not all businesses get it. The following sidebar illustrates the differences between two teams within the wild world of professional baseball, the New York Yankees and the Baltimore Orioles; one team gets it, the other doesn't.

A Tale of Two Teams

Sports fans are probably the most fickle customers on the face of the planet, with many remaining loyal only as long as the franchise fields a winning team. The Baltimore Orioles were once a prime example of a high-quality product, offering fans a wonderful harbor stadium that has become the standard for all new baseball parks, not to mention the appeal of watching super-talented legends such as Cal Ripken.

Over the past decade or so, however, the team's ownership has fired one manager after another, traded player after player, and demonstrated poor leadership. The team's leaders have virtually destroyed the Orioles' fan base. The decline began in 1993 when Peter Angelos headed a group that purchased the team from the bankruptcy-laden Eli Jacobs for $173 million. Angelos was (is) a high-powered attorney who made a fortune representing asbestos victims in class-action lawsuits.

In 1997, the Orioles enjoyed their last winning season. They won 98 games and the AL East title, averaging 45,816 fans per game and 3,711,132 for the entire season (the league's average attendance per team was 2,234,523). In 2007, the Orioles finished in fourth place, averaging just 27,060 fans per game and 2,164,822 for the season.

During the period following the team's purchase, they have had (as of this writing) six managers and six General Managers, and averaged 90 losses per season.

During that same period, the New York Yankees have finished in first place eight times and placed second twice. Until 2008, they had just one manager, Joe Torre, and two GMs. In 1997, the Yankees drew 31,856 fans per game, and 2,580,325 for the season (above the league average but far below the Orioles). In 2007, by contrast, they averaged 52,739 fans per game and 4,271,867 for the season.

The Yankees, George Steinbrenner included, became a model of Team Leadership, consistency and a coherent team process. The Orioles have provided a model of poor leadership, zero consistency and no coherent team process.

Needless to say, each team's fans recognized the difference in the products and responded accordingly by either deserting the stands or flocking to them. The bottom line: you must be the real deal—both to your team members and your clients. This is not a complicated formula.

Assessing Team Member Loyalty

Satisfied personnel are the minimum requirement for delivering Ritz Carlton service with FedEx efficiency—the standards the affluent measure against. A satisfied team member is a *loyal* team member, and loyal personnel are essential for making certain that first-rate service and problem-solving are woven into the team's fabric. This is one of the consistent criteria found among elite teams: *they have loyal team members.* The following graph shows team member satisfaction from our research. As you can see, most but not all team members feel rewarded in their role on the team:

Use the following as a benchmark for factors that can positively or negatively influence team members. The parentheses indicate what each impact factor *should* be:

- Work environment (positive)
- Wealth management services (comprehensive)
- Personnel (good attitude, clear roles, defined areas of responsibility)
- Concept of Kaizen (ongoing improvement)
- Compensation (fair)
- Growth curve (healthy)

If your team cannot respond affirmatively to all of the above, it doesn't mean that your personnel are not loyal. Instead, it suggests that your team members might not be *as* loyal as you'd like, which means your team's service and problem-solving capabilities might have a few gaps.

It's nearly impossible to attract, service and retain wealthy clients when team members are disloyal, disgruntled, inattentive to their work and/or making efforts to jump ship (and take customers with them).

The warning signs of team member dissatisfaction or disloyalty are easy to spot, provided you know what to look for. Watch for team members—as well as Team Leaders—who:

- Focus primarily on their personal needs, ego and/or greed. They are loyal only to themselves, not to others in the organization. Peter Angelos was a perfect example.
- Have a poor work ethic compared to the rest of the team.
- Frequently display an unwillingness to do whatever it takes to complete a task.
- Make minimal contributions to the team and the organization, beyond what the job description calls for.
- Focus on their vacation and sick days, make too many personal phone calls, and/or spend excessive amounts of time emailing friends or surfing the Web.
- Display a lack of initiative; need ongoing instruction for every new task.
- Rarely provide thoughtful ideas that contribute to improving the team.
- Do not interact well with other team members.
- Are not problem solvers; always hand off problems to other team members.
- Become defensive during performance reviews or whenever they're held accountable.
- Have little or no interest in learning or growth.
- Exhibit little concern to the team's business plan and goals.

"Surprise and Delight"

Years ago, I met Jack Laschever, the publisher of *Forbes Life* (formerly *Forbes FYI*), who told a story that illustrates the importance of "surprising and delighting" your best clients.

To celebrate the birth of their new baby, Jack visited Van Cleef & Arpels to purchase a necklace for his wife. As the salesperson discussed his choice, she suggested that he also buy a pair of matching earrings. He declined, but was impressed with her ability to develop a rapport and gather key pieces of personal data.

Five months later, he received a note from this same salesperson, reminding him that his wife's birthday was approaching, and (once again) suggesting the matching earrings as a gift. Then, on the date of his wife's birthday, his wife received a delivery of flowers, with a note from her husband. They were sent by the salesperson from Van Cleef.

I don't know whether Jack will ever buy those matching earrings, but that's not the point. The purpose of "Surprise and Delight" is to strengthen the loyalty of key clients, enhance repeat sales, and gain introductions to potentially *excellent* clients. You also want to build more personal relationships with your best clients, so they become internal advocates—people who will help you gain access throughout the complex.

"Surprise and Delight' isn't about mere gift-giving. It isn't about eliciting a "that's nice" response from clients who receive your fruit basket at Christmas, or an assortment of cheese and summer sausage. It's about collecting as much personal data on your best clients in order to:

- Provide a higher level of service by better understanding their needs and wants.
- Through your gift-giving, impress clients with your understanding of their personal likes and passions.
- Engage the Law of Reciprocity. When you surprise and delight people, you are often rewarded with more business or some other advantage—almost immediately!

Here's how to get started.

Step 1: Uncover the "passion points" of key clients. What personal pursuits are they passionate about—wines, candy, baseball, history, poker, etc.? You should always be thinking about which coffee table books you could send them that would match their interests. They won't throw away a coffee table book that's related to their passion point. Obviously, it doesn't have to be a coffee table book. It can be any item that they're sure to love—within reason.

Step 2: Coordinate your intelligence gathering and gift distribution with your practice manager. It's important that he or she knows when "S&D" packages must be sent, so the candy, wine and collectible baseball cards can be ordered in time.

Everybody gathers personal data simply by engaging in small talk with clients at the beginning or end of meetings and phone calls. Many of you already send gifts to your best clients—here and there.

I'm suggesting you *increase* your intelligence-gathering activities and *systematize* the gift-giving process so that you consistently purchase ideal gifts. If you've ever received tube socks or sweaters as gifts, you already know it takes time and effort to really "Surprise and Delight."

The two junior advisors on Chuck's Founder's Group were not loyal to the team.

They were not honest about their marketing efforts or interactions with clients. Clients were not being serviced properly, which led to their defection. Unfortunately, not enough clients left to capture Chuck's attention, though losing one affluent client is—in my opinion—losing one too many. By the time Chuck realized that his junior advisors, as well as his attractive but incompetent assistant, needed to go, the Human Resource Department demonstrated no loyalty to him. Instead he ran into a "brick wall."

Eventually he was able to make the necessary changes, but HR left such a bad taste in his mouth (the process took nearly six months, totally distracting Chuck and interfering with production), that *his* loyalty to the firm—the only one he'd ever worked for during a 20 year career—was irreparably damaged. Within 18 months, Chuck and his new team were recruited to another firm.

Loyalty is an earned behavior. Effective Team Leaders understand this, and work hard to know their members on a personal level. They combine work, performance-focused accountability and fun. Because they invest time and energy to "get the right people on the bus," their teammates take personal ownership in the team's performance, and are committed both to the team and the team's clients.

It is no coincidence that loyal team members engender loyal affluent clients.

Summary

- Today's affluent clients are looking for "go-to" financial advisors to: coordinate the multi-dimensional aspects of their financial affairs; provide Ritz Carlton service with FedEx efficiency; solve problems quickly and communicate clearly; provide total access to their advisors whenever they want it, and keep them informed at all times.
- Affluent Americans are *very* discriminating. Your products and services had better be as advertised, and you'd better understand that YOU are the chief product.
- Because of the meltdown within the financial world, individual advisors and teams who are capable of delivering the goods will be in more demand.
- Solving a problem quickly and satisfactorily is the most statistically significant criterion strengthening affluent loyalty.
- Two *Performance Factors* are a constant in Elite Financial Teams: 7) affluent client retention; 8) commitment to excellence.
- Elite teams understand the value of loyal clients; they capitalize on the *service-loyalty-revenue nexus.*
- Loyal affluent clients are a financial team's acre of diamonds; they contribute to business development (Rainmaking) with statistical significance.
- NOTHING is more important than ensuring your clients are satisfied, not just at the moment of purchase but forever after.
- The Team Leader builds and maintains a base of loyal, affluent clients by building and maintaining a loyal team. Look for signs of team member dissatisfaction and disloyalty before they impact *client loyalty.*
- Elite teams have statistically higher levels of job satisfaction among team members. This breeds loyalty.

6

Your Wealth Management Process

(Performance Factors 9 &10)

99% of teams provide investment management. Only 84.8% of teams provide a formal financial plan.

—Factoid, Financial Team Research

Mastering the art of selling, servicing and retaining affluent clients requires that you master your deliverables (thoroughly understand your services and products), and respond to the evolving needs of your clientele. When marketing to the affluent, please understand that what you're *really* selling is: (1) your financial team, and (2) your wealth management process.

The financial solutions you offer clients are often out of sight and, therefore, out of mind. Unlike a tangible product such as a computer, television or automobile, which reinforces its value every time it's used (or reminds you that it's a lousy product), stock portfolios, insurance, financial plans and mortgages exist in a world of intangibles. Former Harvard Business Review editor and marketing guru Theodore Levitt puts it best when he says, "the client is never really aware of the value they are receiving until they perceive they did not get what they were promised—until they are dissatisfied." Therefore, "in the intangibles world it is important that you consistently demonstrate, communicate, and quantify your value to each client—to make absolutely sure they are satisfied."

This is why it's easier for elite teams to acquire and service affluent clients. They are better equipped to *consistently* deliver the full array of wealth management services. And let's not forget: elite teams have more eyes and ears to identify and execute "surprise and delight" opportunities. This provides numerous opportunities for elite teams to create dissatisfaction in the minds of affluent prospects about their existing service providers.

Whenever you encounter "loose confederations" of financial professionals posing as teams, odds are that these "teams" are not delivering comprehensive wealth management services. Even when individual advisors have developed strong personal relationships with clients, the clients are probably not getting what they really want or need. Therefore, these clients are vulnerable to the marketing efforts of an elite team. In today's highly competitive world, the baseline expectation is that your team is everything it claims to be.

As mentioned in Chapter 1, our research on the major purchasing decisions of the affluent identified eight primary services that people of wealth seek when selecting a financial advisor or a financial team. The significance of those services in retaining affluent clients has been established in a follow-up survey of affluent investors.

Rather than simply list these statistically significant criteria, I'm going to share the actual printout of a team, using software we developed that benchmarked them against elite teams. Because it is a 40- to 50-page customized assessment, I'll limit my discussion to two statistically significant *Performance Factors.*

Performance Factor #9: Meeting Affluent Client Expectations

Here's a team with three advisors (partners) and three support personnel. Although the partners were aware that they conducted their business differently, it wasn't until they read their team's assessment that they realized how little common ground they shared. It was no wonder that they were losing clients and struggling to acquire new ones.

First, the partners were asked to apply one of the following phrases to each of eight criteria that affluent clients want: (a) Services our Team performs very well to exceptionally well; (b) Services our Team performs moderately well; (c) Services our Team does not perform very well, or (d) Services our Team does not offer.

Feel free to answer the questions yourself, but be brutally honest. (The team's answers are in parentheses.)

1. Helping clients create a comprehensive, formal financial plan. (c)
2. Coordinating investment decisions for clients. (c)
3. Taking steps to understand the client's goals and family situation when giving investment advice. (d)
4. Helping clients select the asset mix for their investment portfolio. (b)
5. Bring in experts to help with financial areas where team members lack expertise. (d)
6. Clearly revealing and justifying your fee structure. (c)
7. Helping clients coordinate and organize all their financial documents. (d)
8. Proactively contacting clients when upcoming tax and other changes will impact their investment portfolio. (b)

I hope you fared better than the three partners. They knew their services weren't aligned with the eight criteria, but had no idea they were so disconnected from the needs of their affluent clients. Unfortunately, too many teams are in the same boat.

The challenge is to make certain that you *always* deliver what the affluent want, and then a little bit more. That requires you constantly improve the delivery of these services.

The best way to approach this is to implement the following *Action Steps* for any area that needs improvement. I recommend you begin with the areas that need the most improvement.

Affluent Client Expectations Action Plan

- Do whatever is necessary to add and deliver any service you don't offer. It's important that you attend to all of your affluent clients' financial needs (six or seven out of eight won't cut it).
- For services you currently provide but that need improvement, be clear on what you offer and exactly *what* you are doing to deliver that service.
- Establish a timeline for improvement—30 days, 60 days or 90 days. The timeline should be based on a realistic assessment of the effort needed to improve delivery of that service.
- Project to the end of your timeline and ask: "What will we need to continually refine? What tasks, if any, should be eliminated? What else should we be doing?"
- Determine how to implement each improvement. Assign responsibility for each element to one individual, and set a deadline.
- Establish how the Team Leader or Practice Manager will monitor improvement efforts. You may want to meet weekly for an update, especially for services that need immediate attention.

Now that we've framed these eight criteria, it's easy to see how every member of an elite team, within his or her specified role, communicates, demonstrates, and quantifies the value delivered by the team—whether that value concerns asset allocation, financial planning, the review process, etc. This is why "surprise and delight" is important to the client loyalty process (see sidebar in Chapter 5). Whenever you do something thoughtful and timely (an anniversary bottle of champagne, a flower arrangement for a birthday), it strengthens the client relationship by demonstrating the *added value of caring.*

The Team IS the Product

This is one of the maxims that Team Leaders of Elite Financial Teams fully comprehend. They recognize that because of the intangible nature of financial solutions, marketing a financial team's deliverables is always a *personal* process. Guided by the Team Leader, every partner (advisor) on the team should be visible in the community. In the intangible world, the reality—from the affluent consumer's perspective—is that each individual representing the team IS the product. This means that the team is only as strong as its weakest link.

In *The Marketing Imagination,* Levitt writes:[5]

> "When prospective customers can't taste, test, feel, smell, watch, or properly try the promised product in advance, the necessity of metaphorical reassurances to the marketing effort become amplified. Promises, being intangible, have to be tangibilized in their presentation . . .
>
> The less tangible the generic product, the more powerfully and persistently the judgment about it is shaped by the "packaging"—how it's presented, who presents it, what's implied by metaphor, simile, symbol, and other surrogates for reality" [which is why Team Leaders of elite teams spend the time, energy, and attention developing their team members].
>
> Intangible products are by nature highly people-intensive in the production and delivery. The more people-intensive a product, the more room there is for personal discretion, idiosyncrasy, error, and delay. Once a customer for an intangible product is sold, the customer can be easily unsold as a consequence of his expectations having been under-fulfilled.

This highlights the importance and the advantages of forming a true Elite Financial Team to market intangible services, develop loyal affluent clients, penetrate clients' centers of influence, stimulate positive word-of-mouth, and develop strategic alliances with other professionals. This also speaks to why such care must be taken to numerous marketing details, since every component forms a sort of "branding mosaic."

Take the oft-misused value statement. Ideally, it should be a simple phrase that clearly encapsulates what the team is all about and what it provides. For instance, "We oversee the financial affairs of a select num-

[5] Levitt, Theodore, *The Marketing Imagination.* New York: The Free Press, 1983, pgs 97 & 98.

ber of families in the area," or "Our team [does the above]," or "I'm in a financial practice that . . . [does the above]."

Because of the intangible nature of wealth management and the complexity of many teams, I've found that a handful of simple questions can become a useful exercise. If you want to have a little fun and be productive at the same time, ask everyone to write out his answer to the following questions:

What does your team do?
What is your team's value statement?
What do you do?
What is your value to the team?

Next, conduct a group discussion, one question and one answer at a time. Unless you have worked through this exercise before, you'll be amazed at the disparity in responses and the confusion regarding one's personal value to the team. Obviously, the objective is to develop a unified response. Reaching that goal can be very challenging, however, and requires real leadership. But eventually, everyone needs to be on the same page.

As Team Leader, it's important to continually remind every member of what defines your team. This is about more than a few words strung together in a value statement. It should become your mantra. Elite teams take this very seriously.

Be sure every team member can articulate this simple statement, naturally and under any circumstances. The statement must accurately reflect what your team REALLY DOES, and should be free of "Shakespearean prose." Too many value statements/ branding messages sound stilted and over-rehearsed when spoken aloud. In addition, many are too complex. By the time the advisor finishes his one-sentence monologue, which took about three minutes to articulate, the prospect's eyes have dimmed because she's mentally "checked out."

A poorly written (and delivered) value statement offers no value to anyone. In fact, it usually hurts your team's branding message, because it comes across like either a Hamlet-style soliloquy or the disingenuous sales pitch of an old-fashioned carnival barker: "Step right up! Get your estate-planning services while they're red hot! Guaranteed to double your beneficiaries' financial potency or your money back!"

Poorly constructed statements, whether in long-winded verse or constructed as a huckster promise, do more than damage your brand. These ill-founded statements create internal confusion, and often produce an adverse impact. They also highlight a lack of clarity regarding team member's individual value to the team.

The Importance of Image

Because your offices, everyone's dress, the automobiles you drive, the use of English (or whichever language is spoken) all contribute to your team's image, it is important that you apply two key concepts:

1. Things that are too flashy and expensive will have affluent clients and prospects thinking, "*You're making too much money.*"
2. Things that are too barren and inexpensive will have affluent clients and prospects thinking, "*You're struggling.*"

Remember, the affluent have middle class values imprinted in their subconscious minds. Although they may live in an 8,000-square-foot house, they will be suspicious of *both* opulence and shabbiness.

You and every team member are the product, so it is important to capture the middle ground, being both upscale and professional. Always pay special attention to the perceptions and biases of today's affluent investors.

For instance, be careful with how often you use the terms "wealth" or "affluent" or "high-net worth." Today's upscale households don't consider themselves wealthy or affluent. They don't refer to themselves that way. Because everyone in the financial services industry is targeting the affluent, and because of the intangible nature of the deliverables, and because claims are made that aren't always credible, the affluent tend to view people using these terms as salespeople. And the affluent DO NOT LIKE salespeople. They really, REALLY don't like salespeople! And they certainly don't like loose confederations of financial professionals posturing as true financial teams! They want the real McCoy, and they are sold by sales skills so refined that they are virtually seamless.

When it comes to the vehicle you and your senior partners drive, the days of owning the most expensive luxury car are long gone. It's fine to drive a luxury car, but avoid purchasing or leasing the biggest and the most expensive Mercedes or BMW. In today's environment, this will create the impression of ostentation.

A few years ago, I met with an advisor at a prominent Wall Street firm who wanted to discuss the pros and cons of forming a financial team. He was finding it more of a challenge than he'd anticipated. I knew I was in for an interesting coaching session when the advisor and his top assistant arrived at my hotel in a Rolls Royce. Since this was my first ride in a Rolls, just a bit pretentious (to say the least), I decided to have a little fun with the advisor. I asked a battery of questions about the Rolls: "How long have you had it? What's the maintenance like? How much does it cost for a tune-up? What kind of gas mileage does it get? What do people think?"

I made my point. By the time we reached his office, he confessed that he bought it after a good year, but was now embarrassed by it. Too many people got the wrong impression. He claimed he'd been trying to sell it, without success.

Well . . . talk is cheap, because his office took pretension into the Twilight Zone. It was enormous! It looked like a Hollywood set designed for Gordon Gecko's richer, more evil twin. It featured dark wood paneling, stuffed animals of every size on every wall (not teddy bears, but once-living animals rendered lifelike by taxidermists), three elegant conference tables, and a fish tank that was larger and contained more species of tropical fish than the Chicago aquarium.

The challenge for this gentleman—we'll call him William—was that he'd hired his assistant, a former administrator of a local hospital, to help him acquire physician clients. It had been nearly a year, and they had only recruited one physician client. The problem involved more than image, but this was where everything began and ended.

Regardless of what he claimed, it was important to William that he demonstrate to every prospect that he made LOTS of money. Everything about him screamed: "I'm rich!" The new assistant tried to convince him to tone it down, and this is where I came into the picture.

William fought me for more than a month after my visit, but I continually stressed that three things get accomplished:

1. William needed to expand his true deliverables and develop a real financial team. Physicians were not looking for an overpaid broker to handle their investments. Like most of today's affluent, they wanted a solutions provider for all aspects of their family's financial affairs. They wanted a "general practitioner of finances."
2. William had to re-define what his team could provide versus what they claimed they could provide in their fancy brochure. They needed a succinct "value statement" everyone could articulate, including the support personnel.
3. William had to stop trying to get physicians to meet in his office. Showing off his "Colonel McBrag-style" office filled with dead mammals (and live fish) was more likely to hurt him than help. This was a big issue. He desperately wanted prospective clients to see the fruits of his success, but for most people, this merely suggested that he suffered from "big ego/ low-self-esteem" syndrome.

At last contact, William was meeting prospective physicians in the hospital cafeteria, and allowed his assistant to lead most meetings. Who knows whether he's been able to keep his ego in check since then, but at least he was trying to change. Because he never directly answered any of my "team questions," my suspicion is that he's still a sole-practitioner playing at being a financial team.

Elite Financial Teams excel at projecting the correct image and, unlike William (who'd become successful in the days of hiring cold-callers and conducting seminars), their Rainmaking skills are solid. Rainmakers excel at cultivating new client relationships. They are the 17% of high-flying solutions providers while the other 83% struggle, the 83% that often rely on slick brochures and marathon-length value propositions.

Now, let's take a look at the other broad and complex *Performance Factor* that defines the wealth management process for elite teams.

Performance Factor # 10: Expanding Categories of Financial Products and Services

Founders Group leader Chuck was an expert in managing money. A Certified Financial Analyst (CFA), he was extremely talented when it came to the stock market. But his team didn't reach the stage of elite status until they expanded the categories of products and services offered. Our research reveals that most financial teams offer three basic categories of financial products and services:

1. Investment (asset) Management.
2. Retirement Planning.
3. Insurance Planning.

Our research also shows that elite financial teams expand their offerings to provide each of these five financial product and service categories:

4. Education Planning.
5. Tax Planning.
6. Charitable Giving Planning.
7. Budgeting and Cash Flow Management.
8. Banking Services.

Our research took an assessment for how many teams offer those services:

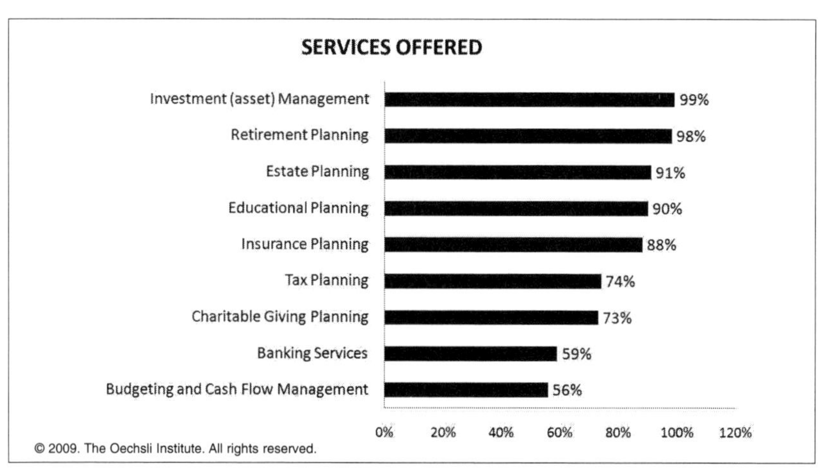

Chuck's team worked the same drill that I used for the three partners above, both for the eight criteria and the expanded products and services. Here's how he took action to improve his offerings: he assigned a team member to a particular area, or he formed an alliance with an outside expert—a "strategic alliance."

Since all of this can be confusing and overwhelming, let me walk you through how Chuck's team initially handled their product and service expansion. I've listed the areas the team was finally able to offer and assigned two codes: "tm"—for team member(s) expertise, and "sa"—for an expert outside of the team, or strategic alliance.

- Alternative Investments / Fixed income specialist (tm)—Ben had dual responsibilities. In addition to being the team's Practice Manager, he was also their alternative investment / bond expert (a by-product of his years of researching investments for Chuck).
- Portfolio management (tm)—Although Ben assists in this area, it is Chuck's area of expertise, which he performs in addition to his role as Team Leader and primary Rainmaker.
- Certified Financial Planner (tm)—Mary is the team's certified financial planner, and her expertise extends to education planning and assisting George in charitable gifting.
- Estate work (sa)—Chuck and Mary developed a strategic alliance with two of the best estate-planning attorneys in the area. They were two of the team's stable of outside experts.
- Insurance (sa)—Mary, the team's CFP, developed a working relationship with a top-flight insurance professional. This individual was both client-friendly and team-friendly (he wasn't trying to steal their clients).
- Real Estate (sa)—Chuck had formed relationships with both a residential and a commercial real estate agent. Though they were outside experts, this was viewed more as a value-added service for affluent clients (and a good referral source).
- CPA (tm & sa)—Although George was a CPA and team member, the Foundations Team didn't sell tax services. However, George had developed strategic alliances with four CPAs. He also han-

dled all the *charitable gifting*. This is another example of an elite team giving the affluent what they want. A "go-to" financial advisor uses outside experts whenever necessary, and the Foundations Team delivered.

- Bankers (tm & sa) –Both Chuck and George developed a healthy working relationship with two bankers, outsourcing all banking services through them. George handled all the *budgeting and cash-flow management* for families wanting that service.

What's interesting to note is that, though the Foundations Team was robust in terms of numbers of partners and expertise, half of the wealth management services they provided were handled by outside experts—banking, estate-planning, insurance, tax services and real estate. The team members (tm) had expertise in five areas—financial planning, portfolio management, alternative investment / fixed income, charitable gifting and budgeting / cash-flow management.

Of course, offering the full array of wealth management services is easier said than done. It took the Foundations Team a year to deliver their expanded wealth management services. Creating strategic alliances requires time and effort, since it's critical that you source experts who meet three criteria, all equal in importance:

- Competency: they must be true experts in their field.
- Client-Friendly: it's essential that every expert is pleasant with clients, and produces quality work in a cost-efficient and timely manner.
- Team-Friendly: it's also essential that your experts are easy to work with, dependable and trustworthy (always supportive of your team and the relationships you have with clients).

Platforms for Success

In today's world of technology, everything may have a similar ring, but not every wealth management platform is equal. I'm not an expert on various technology platforms, but virtually every major firm I've worked with has invested heavily in computer technology including work stations, client databases, investment and performance tracking software, etc. They use this technology to compile and organize the financial information of every client, including managing the portfolios and conducting some form of software driven or web-based planning process (often positioning it as a comprehensive financial plan—when it is not). Some firms, both large and small, have even acquired aggregation tools that let them compile data held at other firms.

Elite Financial Teams will exploit the value of their company's technology platforms only IF they truly provide solutions and communicate clearly with affluent clients. Whenever a tool does not perform up to its internal "PR," top teams take the initiative to invest in their own technology / tools / etc.

Our Financial Team research has provided us with some quick insight into the world of support—by firms and managers:

Top teams get the job done—regardless of their firm or manager—and a good number are independent. If you boil it down to the core, their mission is to *attract, service* and *develop loyal* affluent clients. Everything is about the team and their affluent clients.

Summary

- When marketing to the affluent, understand that what you're really selling is: (1) your financial team, and (2) your wealth management process.
- In the world of intangibles, it's important to consistently demonstrate, communicate, and quantify your value to the clients to ensure they are always satisfied.
- The best financial teams understand the affluent, their needs and wants, and consistently deliver.
- Two *Performance Factors* are consistent in the process of Elite Financial Teams: 9) meeting affluent client expectations (8 Criteria), and 10) expanding categories of financial products and services.
- Elite Financial Teams are true financial teams, not simply marketing entities. They deliver comprehensive wealth management services in a consistent and professional manner.
- The Foundations Team is no exception in the world of elite teams in their use of outside experts. Top teams invest time and effort to establish good working relationships (strategic alliances) with outside experts whenever they have a need.
- A value statement should be a simple phrase that clearly encapsulates what the team is all about and what it provides. For example: "We oversee the financial affairs of a select number of families in the area."
- Each individual team member should be able to articulate his or her value to the team.
- *Everything* that pertains to your team's image is important, because every member of your financial team IS the product. This must be congruent with your wealth management process.
- Attracting, servicing and developing loyal affluent clients is at the core of every elite team. This is hard work.
- There is no cookie-cutter model for developing an elite team.
- Remember: the affluent DO NOT like salespeople!

7

Practice Management

(Performance Factors 11& 12)

> *50% of teams have more than 250 clients; 20% have more than 400 clients.*
>
> —Factoid, Financial Team Research

Good practice management is the basis for jet-fueled operational efficiency.

Remember: When it comes to getting things done cost-effectively and to your clients' total satisfaction, only 17% of your competitors perform at high levels. This is one indicator of the tremendous opportunities awaiting teams willing to "go the extra mile" to capture a larger slice of the affluent market. It's also an indicator that, for most financial teams, practice management tends to be an afterthought, not a daily reality.

Teams with multiple advisors, each handling clients differently, inadvertently create an operational nightmare. Solo advisors sharing an assistant are constantly challenged to obtain enough quality support, and are frequently forced to perform operational tasks that interfere with their ability to schmooze and romance affluent clients.

Our research identified five statistically significant *Performance Factors* (11, 12, 13, 14 & 15) in the practice management of Elite Financial Teams.

- Clear roles and responsibilities.
- Clearly established performance expectations for each role.

- Written procedures that are followed by the team.
- Effectively led team meetings.
- Formal performance reviews.

Practice management is the operating system within a team that determines how things get done, which is why effective Team Leaders often delegate control of practice management. True, some performance factors, such as leading meetings, might involve the Team Leader, but when the Practice Manager assumes more control, it usually leads to a more effective Team Leader.

Because of the depth and breadth of Practice Management, I have devoted two chapters to this component of our team model. This doesn't mean it's more important than the other components, but I want to highlight the numerous bits and pieces involved.

Roles of the Practice Manager

Elite Financial Teams have more in common with well-run dental practices than with the wannabe teams I call "loose confederations." The reason for the dental office analogy rather than a doctor's office is simple: dentists stay on schedule, send out reminders, give away tooth brushes, etc., because they aren't (usually) dealing with life and death issues. They aren't called into emergency rooms, whereas physicians are always, or at least appear to be, running late, dealing with crises, etc.

Elite teams no longer employ sales assistants—in name or reality. Although many firms have changed the title of the sales assistant to "service associate," "client service specialist," "client service associate," etc., these title changes don't necessarily make for operational improvements, as the industry has learned from making the title change from stockbroker to financial advisor to wealth manager.

More than a name change is required. Too many financial advisors still treat support personnel like rental furniture: they're here until I find something better. In effect, they're dispensable, rather than indispensable, sales assistants. Elite teams promote the most capable support people to indispensable practice managers. Their compensation is increased, their responsibilities are expanded, and they are given responsibility for managing subordinate support people (this often includes junior financial advisors).

Barry was the perennial #1 producer at his firm, as well as the leader of an extremely elite team. He contracted my services for two purposes: 1) to re-align his team; and 2) to accelerate his quest for $1 billion in discretionary assets under management. Because his second goal depended on achieving the first, Barry and his assistant Jenny spent two days at our offices in Greensboro, North Carolina.

Unbeknownst to Jenny, Barry had determined that she had the right stuff to become the practice manager he so desperately needed. However, he knew that she would panic at the thought. After the first day of meetings, I met with both of them, highlighted our findings, and offered suggestions.

One suggestion was that Jenny immediately become Barry's practice manager. She turned ashen when I said this. I thought she was going to pass out. Jenny was speechless for a few moments (it felt like minutes), and then timidly protested. She was honored, but the promotion would take her FAR outside her comfort zone. She would have to manage support staff, attend to Barry's needs and oversee daily operations of the entire team.

Within six months, however, she had mastered her new role.

Within two years, she had become indispensable—one of the best practice managers in the entire industry.

Do all teams have a practice manager/ business manager? Should they?

The short answer is: no and yes.

Not all teams have one, but the best teams do.

The most elite financial teams are elevating their best support person to practice manager (also known as a business manager). Heretofore, this was the role of a "sales assistant," and larger producers often had more than one, but they always had a support individual who was indispensable. The best financial advisors use this person to support client relationships and manage the practice, not simply to sell additional stocks and bonds (the old role of a sales assistant).

Sadly, most teams have yet to invest time, energy and resources into creating this role—much less actually hiring or promoting, and then training and delegating a vast array of important responsibilities to these people—responsibilities that can free senior partners to better seek out and service the affluent market.

An Important Team Player

In addition to being an indispensable assistant, the practice manager must be a first-rate utility player with many responsibilities. The following list is incomplete, but gives you a working outline of this indispensable role:

- Supervises support personnel (in some cases, the junior advisors).
- Manages team scheduling, including day-to-day appointments, vacations, holidays, etc.
- Conducts performance reviews of all direct reports (other support personnel).
- Holds all direct reports accountable for performing on a daily basis.
- Solves operational and administrative problems effectively and quickly.
- Has good computer skills; always current with technology.
- Is good with clients.
- Possesses excellent communication skills.
- Possesses excellent organizational skills.
- Has an open mind, with a flexible and problem-solving nature.
- Is an effective delegator; gives small operational tasks to other support personnel.
- Is a life-long learner.
- Consistently exhibits a high level of professionalism.

If this sounds like the job description of an AMAZING person, it is! That's why business managers are crucial to the success of the best teams. Unfortunately, it's easy for mediocre Team Leaders to dismiss the need for such people: "I already have good support. A practice manager will want higher pay for being a glorified office manager."

Is the business manager / practice manager (essentially) an office manager? Yes, but only in the world that looks down on any role that doesn't directly generate revenue.

This is why, while the best teams are setting a trend, most teams won't hire or promote people to practice management status, won't delegate increased responsibilities, and won't pay properly. Therefore, most teams WILL continue to derail themselves through practice management blunders and inefficiencies.

Practice management is often an afterthought, not a daily reality, because it requires work—work to hire and train the right person, which means *replacing* someone if he or she doesn't make the grade.

In addition, our industry still tends to source support personnel from an under-skilled and under-educated talent pool, thanks to the low levels of compensation it's willing to provide. The typical sales associate is hired by a firm for $30,000, and assigned to support two to six financial advisors. (The larger producers get their own assistant.) Thanks to this, the old cliché "you get what you pay for" rings VERY true.

The result is that advisors often feel compelled, and are sometimes instructed, to supplement low base-pay with some form of bonus structure. But this creates further problems. For one thing, most support personnel don't have an entrepreneurial mindset, meaning that whatever bonus/salary arrangement they currently receive becomes an entitlement in their minds. So, it's not uncommon for poor-performing assistants to receive bonuses without any incentive to improve. Worse, until a financial advisor becomes a large producer, he/she has little say in hiring of assistants.

All of this leads to the current dysfunctional system. That said, more and more financial advisors are becoming aware that a good support person (sales assistant) is one of the smartest investments they can make.

Here's another challenge—even if you have a support person who wants to get into the sales side of the business (become an advisor), more often than not, it's because she sees it as her only career path.

She wants the opportunity to make more money and enjoy more respect, hence the idea of embarking on a career as a financial advisor. This is a dangerous path, both for your support person and your team.

Wanting something and having the necessary skill set to succeed are often light years apart. This is especially true in the world of financial services. It's been my experience that the motivation prompting a good support person to become a financial advisor has not been well thought out. The status and money she seeks could probably be satisfied in the role of Practice Manager.

Typically, support personnel in the financial services industry are not given the respect they deserve. Everything revolves around selling. But indispensable assistants like Jenny need to be elevated, in responsibility and compensation, to the role of Practice Manager. With proper guidance and delegation, a formerly indispensable assistant becomes *even more indispensable* as your Practice Manager. I've yet to encounter a Practice Manager on an elite team who wanted to become an advisor.

Barry would have been lost if Jenny decided to become a salesperson. She probably would have struggled, Barry would have been at his wits' end trying to find a suitable replacement, and the performance of his team would have suffered.

Effective Team Leaders are smart businesspeople. They understand the importance of having quality personnel, which is why they invest in support personnel. It's good business!

Performance Factor #11: *Clear* Roles and Responsibilities

The idea here is to create job clarity for each team member. Heretofore, the Team Leader was a successful financial advisor, who often had more of a controlling personality than was productive. Why? She did not trust the quality of her support staff, because her initial experiences with support staff left a lasting negative impression. At earlier stages in her career, she was not able to hire her own support personnel. This was done by the branch manager or firm. Therefore, the typical financial advisor had to share an often-incompetent assistant with three or four other advisors. The result was that financial advisors performed all of the most important tasks themselves. They developed the habit of doing a lot of administrative tasks and smaller client tasks that should have been delegated to *competent* support personnel.

Thanks to all of the above, many financial advisors are suffering from a support personnel hangover. Many a Team Leader gets bogged down, because he fails to delegate properly. But effective Team Leaders are very effective at delegating!

Case in point. A team I'll call KPG was led by a gentleman named Bob. In order to excel at Rainmaking, Bob knew he needed to spend *much* more time with top clients. But he never seemed to have the time . . . for three reasons:

1. He was a CFP who personally created and updated financial plans for each of his clients—each and every one.
2. He had too many clients, and was reluctant to delegate relationship management of his Gold Level clients (second tier) to a junior advisor. He had been burned before. (Earlier, he'd taken on a junior advisor and delegated smaller clients to him, but the advisor soon wanted more money, and when he didn't get what he wanted, left KPG for another firm and tried to "steal" the clients.)
3. The leader meddled in practice management issues, because his nature was to be a "control freak."

This changed radically—and radical change is essential for real change. Bob and I determined that his face-time with top clients, with their centers-of-influence, his strategic alliances and/or affluent prospects was a $2,000 to $2,500-per-hour activity. Meanwhile, working on a financial plan was $50-dollar-an-hour work, and managing his practice was a $35 per-hour job. Suddenly, Bob worked feverishly to get all non-$2000 to $2500-per-hour work off of his plate. He wanted to spend 75% to 80% of his time engaged in the big-money activities.

To do this, he:

1. Elevated his assistant to practice manager, and increased her pay and areas of responsibilities. She, in turn, eliminated all of her tasks that were not $35-an-hour tasks, and identified those that were only $10 to $15-per-hour clerical tasks. This required reconfiguring responsibilities for a second support person.
2. Hired a planner (an advisor with a CFP) for a dual role: to generate all the financial plans and handle all Gold-Level clients.
3. Agreed to give away clients that fell below his Gold Level, which constituted more than 150 relationships.

The irony of having been a control freak is that Bob had to give up some control in order to gain REAL control over his entire team. Today, his team is functioning at a much higher level of performance, he's less stressed, and he's empowered two key players (his practice manager and financial planner) whose roles previously did not exist.

This is an example of matching the roles and responsibilities within your team to improve three key areas: 1) practice management by creating the role of practice manager; 2) wealth management by hiring a CFP to handle all planning and oversee the team's wealth management process, and 3) Team Leadership through delegation that enabled Bob to spend more time Rainmaking.

Prior to these radical changes, Bob was leading a very professional financial team that was extremely client-centric, had two clearly established levels of service, and was delivering a high-quality product. Yet, he was not getting much penetration into clients' centers-of-influence. Sure, Bob would get the occasional referral, but it wasn't what he expected relative to the quality of services provided.

In Bob's previous life as a Team Leader, he was a technician. Not only did he keep total control over the financial planning process, he also got much too involved in areas that should have been delegated.

Our research is crystal clear on this point: the affluent don't want a technician managing their relationships and overseeing their financial affairs. They want a "go-to" coordinator—someone who can vet the technicians as needed. Affluent clients will gladly introduce you to family members, friends and colleagues if you have the skills of a Rainmaker. What this means is that you, the Team Leader, must aggressively delegate practice management to have time to proactively penetrate your top clients' centers-of-influence.

This is the playing field where the $2,000 to $2,500-per-hour activities live. Once Bob gave himself permission to delegate, a major out-of-comfort zone decision, he freed up time to spend with top clients. Once he began spending time with his top clients, he began to understand the importance of improving his sales skills; he knew he was in the midst of serious opportunities, but that he'd better not come across like a salesman. Once he began to work on his sales skills (he attended a Rainmaker Weekend), the time he was spending with his top clients took on a different meaning. Bob was able to engage in two powerful high-priority activities simultaneously: strengthen his team's relationship with top clients and uncover Rainmaking opportunities. New relationships began to enter his team's pipeline.

Within three months of enacting these changes, Bob brought in four new affluent relationships and $9 million in new assets. And the best part is: he's only just begun!

Before moving to the next *Performance Factor,* you might find the following **4-step process** helpful in organizing your team's areas of responsibilities.

4-Step Area of Responsibility Process

1. Determine who will assume the LEAD ROLE for that area. Depending on the size and makeup of your team, you may decide to have more than one team member assume a Lead Role (Team Leader and senior partner jointly assume responsibility for affluent client management and Rainmaking).
2. Assign specific FIXED DAILY ACTIVITIES (FDAs) to the Lead Role, with priority emphasis given to those FDAs that he is best

able to perform. The idea is to empower while capitalizing on core competencies.

3. List the rest of the FDAs to be performed in that area under the Support Fixed Daily Activities category.
4. Identify potential coordination problems and what you will do to prevent them.

The idea is that everyone agrees on two things:

- The specific Fixed Daily Activities and which tasks should be under each Area of Responsibility. This will take some time, but it's worth it.
- Exactly what's involved in performing each Fixed Daily Activity you select.

My suggestion is to always strive for clarity. Even though we are discussing Practice Management, all five components of our Elite Team Model need to be included as you organize roles and areas of responsibilities.

In the following boxes I have provided simple examples for the Team Leader and Practice Manager.

1. Team Leader Box A

   Responsible for: Business Development (Rainmaking), establishing individual performance expectations, individual accountability, managing select client relationships, inspiring and directing the team to achieve its goals.

   Include FDAs in such areas as:
   - Contacting 5 top clients.
   - Meeting with 2 top clients, prospects, or centers-of-influence.
   - Source one potential prospect name from top client's center-of-influence.
   - Meet with Practice Manager.
   - Find someone on the team doing something well and recognize them.

- Surprise & Delight Ideas—e.g., sending a commemorative Shea Stadium T-shirt to a top client who is a die-hard Mets fan.

2. Practice Management Box B
   Responsible for: Overall operational efficiency of the team, with the objective of consistently delivering Ritz Carlton-quality service with FedEx-level efficiency.

   Include FDAs in such areas as:
   - Preparing and updating Financial Organizers for affluent clients—e.g., preparing the Financial Organizer for the advisor to review prior to a client review.
   - Scheduling Client Reviews—e.g., contacting top clients, sending out review announcements and reminders.
   - Making certain that every step of the wealth management process meets current compliance requirements—e.g., review outgoing correspondence, double-check all transactions.
   - Organizing and maintaining an adequate filing system—e.g., keep files current on a daily basis.
   - Establish performance and service standards—e.g., develop Gold and Platinum service models, assign clients to a model, and then handle client questions, complaints and requests accordingly.
   - Schedule team meetings—e.g., hold daily huddles with Team Leader and organize weekly team meetings.
   - Schedule support personnel meetings—e.g., daily huddle with support staff and organize weekly meeting.
   - Handling inner-company reports, correspondence, complaints and other paper flow—e.g., making certain correspondence is current and handled properly.
   - Maintaining computers, office equipment, phone systems, supplies and other administrative support systems—e.g., back-up database in afternoon.

Performance Factor #12: Establishing and Meeting Performance Expectations

Once roles and responsibilities have been established, the next step is to establish performance expectations. Each standard should establish a clear expectation within that critical area.

In the Appendix, I've included three worksheets that many teams have found useful in developing clear performance standards: a *Performance Standards Worksheet,* a *Monitor Compliance Standards Guideline* and a *Create Master Schedules Guideline.* All three can become part of the written procedures in a team manual.

Meeting performance expectations goes hand-in-hand with assigning the right roles and responsibilities to the right people. As you define performance expectations, consider how well your team uses each other's knowledge and abilities when assigning roles and responsibilities (*Performance Factor # 11).*

All of this lies within the responsibility of the Team Leader and Practice Manager—and it takes work. Because people are creatures of habit, expect some resistance when you first establish performance expectations and accountability measures. The following assessment should help you in establishing and meeting performance expectations:

Performance Expectations Assessment

4—Strongly Agree, 3—Agree, 2—Somewhat agree, 1 - Disagree

1. Team Leader is fully committed to the team's long-range business plan and annual goals.
2. Each individual team member is committed to the team's long-range business plan and annual goals.
3. Individual team members have clear roles and areas of responsibility.
4. Individual team members have a clear understanding of their roles, areas of responsibility and performance expectations.

5. Whenever a team member underperforms and resists being held accountable to performance expectations he is replaced.
6. Team Leader and Practice Manager meet quarterly with their direct reports to review performance and communicate team goals.
7. Individual accountability (including Team Leader) is incorporated into the weekly team and support staff meetings.
8. Everything is done right the first time.
9. Everything is clear and understandable to the client.
10. Clients always receive knowledgeable and helpful assistance from your team.
11. Everything is delivered to the client when and where they need it.
12. Your team always keeps promises to clients.
13. Everything is customized to each client's unique needs and wants.
14. Your team continually finds new ways to serve each client's particular needs.
15. Clients perceive that the value your team provides justifies the fees they pay.

Scoring:

45—60 You are doing an excellent job inspecting what you expect in terms of performance expectations. Strive to continue improving your performance at all levels.

30—44 Although performance expectations are being met in many areas, things are still slipping through the cracks. With a little more emphasis on performance expectations, your team will experience immediate and positive results.

< 30 Your team has a lot work to do. It's time to start leading and driving performance at every level. Team Leader and Practice Manager must step-up and take ownership!

After scoring your team using the assessment above, it is easy to see why most teams avoid this entire process. It's tough to be so brutally honest, which is why most teams usually get lost somewhere in the Storming-Norming trap. Since everything should be geared to serving the affluent, the following helpful guidelines have been gleaned from our research. Think in terms of minimum performance expectations for every role, area of responsibility and task.

Summary

- When it comes to getting the job done cost-effectively, and to your clients' total satisfaction, only 17% of your competitors (teams) are making the grade. This presents tremendous opportunities!
- The Practice Manager's role is indispensable in elite teams. Whenever possible, an effective Team Leader elevates his most capable support person into this role.
- Practice Managers' compensation is increased commensurate with their expanded roles and increased responsibilities (which include managing people).
- *Performance Factors* 11 and 12 are consistently found within elite teams (11—clear roles and responsibilities; 12—clear performance expectations).
- Delegation is essential to effective practice management.
- Performance expectations must be clear and team members must be held accountable, including the Team Leader.
- Be like Bob! Team Leaders need to spend 70% to 80% of their time on the $2,000 to $2,500 activities: either face-to-face with the affluent or leading their teams.

8

Practice Management

(Performance Factors 13, 14 & 15)

> *Elite teams are more likely to report that they have written systems and procedures.*
>
> —Factoid, *Financial Team Research*

It's not my intention to overwhelm you with Practice Management, but there are lots of bits and pieces to comprehend—many moving parts to scrutinize. You can compare these two chapters on practice management tools and processes to the most complete toolkit sold by Sears. It can be intimidating, and there will be more tools than you can use at any one time. However, you will have virtually every tool you need . . . when you need it.

In that spirit, let's get started on *Performance Factor 13.*

Performance Factor # 13: Written Policies and Procedures

Elite teams function like successful small businesses, and their Team Leaders know what it takes to function like profitable small businesses. They put policies and procedures in place that every team member must embrace and adhere to. This is not an option, but an expectation.

Too many teams propose policies and procedures that aren't fully embraced, which means they aren't driven by the Team Leader and, consequently, the team's level of efficiency isn't consistent. Little things fall through the cracks, and at times, so do big things.

Elite Financial Teams establish and closely follow written procedures for at least six key processes:

- Launching a new client relationship.
- Providing ongoing client service.
- Scheduling and conducting client reviews.
- Providing operations and administrative support.
- Planning and conducting team meetings.
- Meeting compliance requirements.

The idea of creating a FedEx standard is to put processes and systems in place that are linked to high efficiency and customer service. Everyone pitches in to get the job done in a timely manner, and is always striving to improve. However, it is essential that you are clear about which procedures your team has established.

One ingredient found in all elite team "mixes" is the Japanese concept of Kaizen—ongoing improvement. This is not to say that every procedure must be handled with FedEx speed, but rather that every procedure has a specific workflow process attached to it. When responding to a client problem, our research on the affluent tells us that solving the problem quickly, communicating clearly and making absolutely certain that the client understands and is okay with the solution, is the #1 Criterion for strengthening loyalty. According to the FedEx Standard, the client needs to make just one phone call to resolve a problem quickly, regardless of which team member receives the call.

Another simple concept is return calls: the FedEx standard for returning calls from affluent clients is typically within two hours. If that proves impossible, then another team member returns the call to explain the unusual circumstances. Gold Level (more on this shortly) clients usually receive return calls within 24 hours.

This speaks to another FedEx standard employed by Elite Financial Teams: establishing two distinct tiers of service. There is a top level I refer to as the "Platinum Level" and a second tier I call the "Gold Level." The Platinum Level clients get top-shelf treatment while Gold Level customers receive good service and a strong level of efficiency, but the Gold Level standard is somewhat lower. I have provided examples of both in the bulleted lists below. (The figures in the parentheses are merely a guideline. You must determine your own revenue levels.)

Platinum Level

Ideal clients (generating > $15,000 annual revenue)

- 24/7 access: personal cell phone of Team Leader and practice manager.
- Quarterly Reviews: in-person or by teleconference, client's choice.
- Annual Review: in person.
- Quarterly Intimate Client Event Invitation: wine tasting, sporting event, theater, golf outing, etc.
- Weekly Touch (personal telephone contact) with a team member.
- Bimonthly dinner with the Team Leader.
- Birthday event for one spouse.
- Direct telephone access: two-hour return phone call limit if the individual the client is trying to reach is unavailable.
- Comprehensive Wealth Management Services (Chapter 6): delivered with Ritz Carlton-quality service and FedEx efficiency.

Gold Level

Profitable but not ideal clients (between $4,000–$14,999 annual revenue)

- Access to team during workday business hours.
- Semi-annual reviews: teleconference or with junior partner.
- Quarterly contact: telephone call from junior advisor.
- Monthly service contact: call from a support person.
- Holiday cards: personalized but automated.
- Birthday cards: personalized but automated.
- Same workday return phone call.
- Wealth Management Services as they apply: financial plan, etc.

The challenge many teams encounter is offering too many levels of service: A-client service, B-client service, C-client service, D-client service, etc., which creates tremendous internal confusion and inefficiencies. More often, mediocre teams provide a "one-size-fits-all" standard, which results in no real standard. Things always fall through the cracks, and top clients rarely get the level of attention they deserve.

Your Team Manual

Imagine that your team's practice management is part of the ISO 9000, a family of standards for quality management systems. ISO 9000 is maintained by ISO, the International Organization for Standardization, and is administered by accreditation and certification bodies. Like all companies that are part of ISO 9000, your team would be independently audited and certified to ensure conformance, which would then allow you to say that your team is ISO 9000 certified. Before that point, however, your auditor would ask for your team manual, and also check for:

- a set of procedures that covers all key processes in the business
- monitoring processes to ensure they are effective
- adequate record-keeping
- quality assurance—checking output for defects, with appropriate and corrective actions taken when necessary
- regular reviews of individual processes and the quality system itself and
- facilitation of continual improvement.

ISO 9000 and Total Quality Management (TQM) might be a bit much for a financial team. However, any team should be able to pass a modified audit, where your team manual affirmatively answers the following questions:

Financial Team Audit

4—Yes, absolutely, 3—Yes, but not always documented, 2—Sort of (work in progress), 1– No

1. Current long-range Business Plan that is committed to writing.
2. Annual and quarterly Metrics Scorecards linked to Business Plan.
3. Individual job descriptions are complete, with clear roles and responsibilities.
4. Clear performance standards and review process for each role.
5. Master calendar that includes office hours, team schedule, client reviews, client events, individual performance reviews, weekly team meetings, team activities and events, individual vacations, etc.
6. Practice Management policies and procedures: clear and in writing.
7. Problem resolution procedures (solving client problems): clear and documented.
8. Value proposition in writing.
9. Wealth Management Process: detailed and in writing (includes all client services and solutions).
10. Platinum and Gold client service guidelines: clear and in writing.
11. Client profile: ideal and minimum that is documented.
12. Client Loyalty Process: clear and in writing.
13. Team organizational chart: current and documented.
14. Accurate, current, and accessible record keeping.
15. Team Manual that includes all of the above documents, with a copy in the possession of each team member.

Scoring Key:

45—60 Your team is doing a terrific job! Keep up the good work in the spirit of ongoing improvement, and improve whenever necessary.

30—44 Your practice management is at a tipping point. With a little work, it could be very good, but if neglected, you might

	not pass your next audit. Work to improve any area in which you scored less than 3.
< 30	Your team has serious work ahead. Both Team Leader and Practice Manager need to get busy or your team is going to face serious challenges in the world of the affluent.

Depending on how your team scored on this audit, you can add whatever you like to this manual. The idea is straightforward. For example, if a new person joins your team, she is given a copy of your manual, and within a few days, should have a working knowledge of your team that would otherwise take months to acquire. The manual will also accelerate the process of a new team member developing into a productive player.

Each of the previous practice management performance factors has helped create the framework for:

Performance Factor #14: Leading Team Meetings

The best financial teams not only conduct regular team meetings, they utilize these meetings to make certain everyone communicates what has occurred since the last meeting, what is about to occur, what needs immediate attention within their area of responsibility, as well as problems that need to be solved. Individual accountability is a theme woven throughout the fabric of every effective meeting.

There are two dimensions to an effective team meeting:

1. Meeting Content—the idea is to make certain your team meetings are the venue for . . .

    - Reviewing the past week.
    - Discussing the upcoming week.
    - Solving problems.
    - Making important decisions.

- Assigning responsibility for solving specific problems *and* implementing specific solutions.
- Providing accountability, feedback and support on a personal level.

2. Meeting Structure—there are five key elements that serve as the framework for leading an effective team meeting . . .

   - Starting and ending meetings on time.
   - Providing a stated purpose for each meeting.
   - Providing an agenda for each meeting.
   - Ensuring that key decisions are recorded.
   - Ensuring that actions on decisions are taken following the meeting.

Few people like meetings, because most are mind-numbing wastes of time that are not planned or conducted properly. This is the main reason why many financial teams don't meet on a consistent basis.

It should come as no surprise, therefore, that Elite Financial Teams conduct *effective* meetings, and do so consistently. They don't waste time. They are paragons of efficiency. Elite teams are religious about holding their team meetings. At minimum, these teams meet once a week at a set time.

Many top teams go one step further. The support personnel meet alone with the Practice Manager prior, usually the day before, the weekly team meeting. Following the same format for holding effective meetings allows the support personnel to have open and honest discussions that might have been tempered by the presence of the Team Leader. Naturally, the outcome of these meetings becomes part of the agenda for the weekly team meeting.

Not only do these crème de la crème teams meet on a consistent basis, most conduct quarterly off-sites and annual retreats. A quarterly off-site may sound grandiose, but it's simply a way to get the entire team out of the office to review their metrics and scorecards, and to discuss other relevant performance factors. The *annual retreat* is far more involved, often entailing a full weekend, whether at a Team

Leader's holiday home or a local resort. Here, everything is discussed—from the annual metrics scorecard (goals), to roles and responsibilities, to interpersonal relationships, and more. These annual retreats are so powerful that I've included a chapter at the end of the book outlining an ideal retreat, with team exercises that might prove helpful.

Although Team Leaders usually lead team meetings, practice managers often control the schedule for all meetings (team and support), make certain meetings are held, and are proactive about tracking attendance. In other words, they make all the meetings function. A strong practice manager is an integral member of an Elite Financial Team.

In the Appendix you will find a *Suggested Meeting FORMAT,* a *Team Meeting Planning Checklist* and a *Team Meeting Evaluation Form.* These provide a "no surprises" element to help all team members participate, contribute, and leave every meeting with specific action items.

Performance Factor #15: Formal Performance Reviews

Regardless of your team's stage of development, it's important to formally review each member's performance. This is an arena where elite teams actively apply the concept of Kaizen. Although you may view your team as a functional unit, where all members are focused on achieving common goals, there is a natural tendency for three things to happen that can negatively affect operational efficiency:

- Team members continue to do what they've always done, trying to balance team goals with their old ways of doing things. This creates a challenge when it comes to integrating and coordinating efforts toward attracting, servicing and developing loyal affluent clients.
- The Team Leader and other senior players don't agree on, and coordinate, the delegation of tasks. This leads to inefficiency. Team Leaders and senior partners perform tasks that prevent them from spending time with affluent clients and their centers-of-influence. Meanwhile, support personnel are not empowered to

expand their areas of responsibility, and they perform tasks on a reactive basis.

- The Team Leader and other senior team members delegate tasks, not areas of responsibility, and fail to inspect what they expect. Consequently, tasks are performed with little thought as to how they fit into the overall operation, let alone the long-range business plan.

Financial teams that have reached the elite stage consistently conduct formal performance reviews for each team member. There are 7 key elements that largely determine the quality of these performance reviews:

1. Scheduling performance reviews . . . annually or more frequently.
2. Linking individual team performance to team goals.
3. Focusing on performance, not personality.
4. Praising exceptional and acceptable performance.
5. Uncovering reasons for poor performance.
6. Emphasizing growth and development.
7. Monitoring ongoing efforts to improve performance.

Until areas of responsibility become clear, it's difficult for team members to coordinate and integrate their efforts with one another. Whether the Practice Manager, Team Leader or Junior Partner reviews the support personnel, it's important to focus on Fixed Daily Activities (FDAs). Granted, certain activities don't need to be scrutinized on a daily basis, but only when team members perform all of their tasks, especially FDAs, does coordination become possible.

Streamlining Procedures & Reducing Time Wasters

There will be situations where one team member's area of responsibility will require that tasks be assigned to another team member. In these instances, efficiency challenges can occur, and it may be necessary to bring these team members together to streamline their procedures. For example, one individual might have the responsibility for updating a client's Financial Organizer while another is responsible for creating performance review statements. Since these performance review statements are part of the updated Organizer, it might be more efficient if the team member updating the Financial Organizer is also responsible for the performance review statements.

This requires both individuals to communicate clearly and not get into any "turf" protection, which can easily happen. The following is a process that can be helpful whenever you discover procedures that need to be streamlined.

Streamlining Procedures

1. Team member(s) responsible are to describe the procedure and the objective that it's designed to achieve.
2. Team member(s) list the procedure steps in sequence, noting who is responsible for each step.
3. Practice Manager or Team Leader works with team member(s) to evaluate the procedure as follows:

    - Eliminate Duplication. Are tasks being performed by two different team members, or at different times in the procedure? A common inefficiency is for the same information to be gathered or generated by different people at different times.
    - Combine Tasks. Here, you want to look for opportunities to take two different tasks and combine them, having one team member perform them as a single task.
    - Simplify a Task. This is an ongoing challenge in my office. If we're not careful, things get more complicated than necessary. You want to discuss how each task is performed. If it sounds confusing, it is. Help the individual responsible for that task find ways to simplify it, which will reduce the time required to perform it.

- Eliminate a Task. Be on the lookout for opportunities to eliminate one or more tasks that do not add value to the procedure. Frankly, this is where our office is most guilty. Because we have so many things going on at the same time, we are always on the lookout for "busy work." Get rid of busy work!
- Eliminate "White Space." Look for paperwork that sits in someone's in-basket, waiting for attention. Establish a protocol for staying on top of your paper-flow.
- Checklists. Whenever you can create a checklist for a task, you've created leverage. Other people can perform the task, and will reduce time and errors.
- Errors. Whenever there is any ongoing mistake that has not been eliminated, or things are being overlooked, the Practice Manager should determine what is causing the error, and come up with ways to eliminate the cause.

4. Practice Manager and/or Team Leader then lists the revised procedure steps and assigns responsibility for each.
5. Practice Manager and/or Team Leader reviews progress in 30 days.

In the Appendix you will find a *Streamlining Procedures Checklist* that we use in our workshops. Teams we've worked with have found it helpful.

I have yet to discover a team that did not benefit from periodically focusing on reducing time wasters. With a little effort, a team can save between 4 and 12 hours of wasted activity each week. Have each team member read *Common Time Wasters* in the Appendix. This is a good semi-annual team drill.

Summary

- Five of the 15 *Performance Factors* are consistently found in the Practice Management Process of elite teams: 11) clear roles and responsibilities, 12) clear performance expectations, 13) written procedures, 14) effective team meetings, and 15) formal performance reviews.
- Elite teams often offer two levels of service, depending on clients' investable assets—usually "Platinum Level" and "Gold Level" packages. These service levels are clearly defined.
- The best teams have a manual, containing everything from their business plan and annual goals to roles and responsibilities, specific procedures, etc. Think in terms of passing an ISO 9000 audit.
- Conducting well-run team meetings is an essential component of a team. These meetings need to be consistent, time sensitive, and have an agenda.
- Practice Managers in many elite teams conduct weekly meetings for the support personnel prior to the weekly team meeting.
- Quarterly reviews and annual retreats strengthen team camaraderie and keep everyone focused on the team's goals.
- Performance reviews are a vital component of accountability. Both the Team Leader and Practice Manager should conduct (at minimum) *annual* performance reviews with their direct reports.
- Always work to eliminate time wasters, and streamline procedures (eliminate duplication).

SECTION III

Myths and FAQs

9

Common Myths

The affluent are different—Myth; 93% are self-made—Fact.
—Factoid, Affluent Research

MYTH: Teams are glamorous and more likely to attract the wealthiest clients.

REALITY: It's all Goldman Sachs' fault. Their success with teams, combined with their panache, has made teams glamorous. Everyone wants to be like Goldman Sachs. Every financial advisor wants to position and market their wares on the level of Goldman Sachs. Once it became known that Goldman was using the team approach in their sales process, forget the details: *everyone* wanted to form a team to compete in marketing against Goldman.

I'm not sure who originally thought that the "be like Goldman" mania would enable teams to become glamorous marketing juggernauts. But it's a common misconception, often among solo financial advisors who have yet to actually form or join a team. Often, these misguided souls look forward to the support and camaraderie of colleagues. In their minds, they will get support, share ideas, and receive a needed boost in confidence by marketing themselves as a team. Affluent people prefer teams. Goldman's success is proof positive, right? Life will be good.

Our research on the affluent and on teams tells us that:

- The affluent are looking for a "go-to" solutions provider.
- Elite teams excel at attracting, servicing, and developing loyal affluent clients, because among other things, they are better able to address the full array of needs and wants of today's affluent investor.
- Only 17% of the financial teams are performing at optimum levels. The majority are stuck in a *Norming-Storming* trap.
- A sole practitioner who creates a strong strategic alliance with specialists can also meet the needs of the affluent very well, though it's more difficult.
- Most teams are not properly formed. They rush to get started, which is like rushing into marriage. Teams are like a business marriage: easy to form and challenging to make work.

MYTH: Team dynamics, clear roles, business plans, etc. are all overrated.

REALITY: Absolutely not! Although elite teams are rare, they deserve all the accolades they get. What *is* overrated are teams that produce strong numbers because of a select few members. I'm sure you've seen it happen: a couple of successful advisors combine their businesses, and collectively, their numbers are strong. In reality, however, they are two independent advisors operating under the guise of a team. Or, you might have seen a second-generation team: a son and son-in-law take over daddy's business. For a time, the numbers are strong, but when the data is benchmarked against our research, these teams are not elite status. Why? For a number of reasons . . .

First, odds are that they are no longer in growth mode, which is an essential component of elite teams. Second, there is usually a serious leadership void. The number one criterion that has surfaced from our research highlights Team Leadership as the essential ingredient. Effective leadership must be developed and earned. It cannot be assigned.

MYTH: "I can do everything better myself, within my current areas of expertise."

REALITY: Maybe so. But is it best to devote your time and energy to low-paying administrative and Practice Management activities that could be handled by an intelligent Practice Manager, who then can delegate lesser tasks to another support person? Revisit the examples in Chapter 7 on $2,500-per-hour activities versus $50 to $35 to $15-per hour tasks.

Bottom line: it's extremely difficult, if not impossible, to serve the affluent by going it alone. It takes a team. If you are solo, that means developing a virtual team—a group of experts who serve as your "think tank" for affluent clients. If you're serious about maximizing your potential, divest yourself from $15 to $50-per-hour tasks.

MYTH: "We're doing well as a team, we all get along, we have roles and responsibilities that we're comfortable with, so why tamper with perfection?"

REALITY: Such comfort and perfection are usually illusions fostered by people rationalizing why their team is stuck in the *Norming* stage of development. If there is no drive by the Team Leader to grow the business or improve performance, the emphasis is typically on "let's all get along." This phase is deceptive, because it often mirrors elite status without achieving it.

Because it's in human nature to gravitate to others, and because the old world of stockbrokers is a rather lonely endeavor, advisors like the idea of being part of something bigger. The idea of peer support, camaraderie, and colleagues leaning on each other is compelling.

Extraordinary human qualities exhibited in athletics or in a crisis quickly evaporate within the world of a financial team that is not serious about growth. After all, the weaker links (non-contributing team members) can cover their shortcomings for a longer period in a plateaued team.

MYTH: "We're doing everything right, because we adhere to the Kaizen concept of continuous improvement."

REALITY: If your team is truly adhering to Kaizen, you wouldn't express an attitude that reeks of complacency. Effective teams are always fine-tuning what they do; always looking to improve. Whenever I've benchmarked a strong team against best practices, they are always more critical of themselves than a team in the *Norming Stage.* When teams actually embrace Kaizen, they are improving their Rainmaking, systems, technology, service, etc., and not resting on the laurels of "doing everything right."

This is a serious Achilles heel. It's naïve to assume that, because your team is committed to continuous improvement, it has automatically entered the coveted league of elite teams. This is analogous to an athlete who performs well in practice, but disappears during the game. In the world of athletics, game-time performance is all that counts. The same is true for elite teams.

Whenever a team gets caught-up in mastering process at the expense of growth, it's no different than the athlete excelling in practice but not during the pressures of a game. I will always remember Jack, a Team Leader who spent two years making certain that his team had policies and procedures for everything. In fact, he had triplicate procedures for many of his client-service initiatives. When I finally talked with him, he spent 95% of our conversation telling me about the exceptional quality of his team's processes. It was only after I asked him "why" he called that he confessed: "We haven't brought in the quantity of new affluent clients that we deserve." Process, in and of itself, does not guarantee growth.

Improvement that is not directly linked to a clear and measurable goal is incomplete, at best. At worst, it means you are avoiding the cruel world of winning and losing, and have resigned yourself to being a "practice player." Elite teams are like Tiger Woods: they practice hard and often, but their main goal is to win.

MYTH: Big numbers = a healthy team.

REALITY: The research is clear: all things being equal, a team is healthy when it's in serious growth mode and has embraced all 15 *Performance Factors.* This means that your team is excelling at Rainmaking (developing one loyal affluent client after another) and delivering comprehensive wealth management services. Bottom-line: the team is providing high-level solutions for its affluent clients. Big profits in the short term mean . . . well, big profits in the short term, which is good, as long as those numbers aren't subject to a quick reversal because the team has *not* reached a high-performing stage.

MYTH: Longevity = a healthy team.

REALITY: This may or may not be true. Some teams survive for long periods because their leaders reinvent them generation after generation. Others, especially family teams, get stuck in purgatory—the *Storming-Norming* trap.

Although longevity is a sign of success for Galapagos tortoises and Redwood trees, consider the Chicago Cubs. This team is one of the oldest in Major League Baseball, but hasn't won a World Series title since 1908. Is this a healthy team? In my opinion: no. If the Cubs were a less storied team in a smaller market, they would have been relocated or disbanded decades ago. (Side note: I'm a baseball fan, and just once would like to see the Cubs win it all.)

A long-lived team is usually winning on a consistent basis. Remember, job satisfaction and team growth go hand in hand. In all likelihood, if a team has been together for a long time, and is not stuck in purgatory, it's probably a healthy team that will continue to grow.

MYTH: Teams are an easier way to succeed than going solo.

REALITY: Because they are like families, teams require work, which often means sacrificing what you (as a member or leader) would prefer to do with your time—e.g., play business golf on a Saturday rather than go to your in-laws for lunch / attend the team quarterly half-day offsite meeting on Friday rather than go to a neighborhood social function, etc. But with sacrifice comes the reward of not having to do everything yourself. Having more than one person capable of solving client problems makes life easier. Having everyone on the team schmooze affluent clients makes your life easier. But there is NO free lunch. There are trade-offs, but nobody on an *elite team* would have it any other way.

MYTH: "Once we learn how to work together, we'll leave conflict behind."

REALITY: This is a common misconception and the reason why most teams hover in the *Storming-Norming* trap. They naively assume that when everyone gets along, everything will be okay. Not so! Conflict will creep in whenever a leader is not driving team growth. Roles and responsibilities will subtly and (later) blatantly get questioned. Team members will start mumbling about others' contributions, and they will bicker over compensation. Before you know it, you'll return to the *Storming* stage again.

Summary

- Much of the information circulating about teams contains bits-and-pieces of truth, but the facts are usually missing.
- Make no mistake about it—Elite Financial Teams excel in attracting, servicing, and developing loyal affluent clients.
- Elite Teams require hard work.
- Neither the number of team members nor the level of production guarantees an Elite Financial Team.
- Elite teams have incorporated the 15 *Performance Factors* which contributes directly to both their overall health and growth curve.

10

Frequently Asked Questions

27.8% of teams use small client events (with clients bringing guests) as part of their core marketing strategy.

—Factoid, Financial Team Research
and Rainmaker Research

To start the Frequently Asked Questions chapter, I thought it would be helpful to field some questions from a leading financial team expert, Dr. Richard Orlando. Dr. Orlando is an industry veteran, heading the Practice Management group for a major financial institution. His expertise in the world of financial teams is highly regarded, to say the least. Dr. Orlando asked the following questions after reading an advance copy of this book.

When Matt asked me to write a short passage for his new book, I was both honored and quite curious to see what he had learned about Elite Financial Advisor Teams. I was curious because I have read many books on teams (let alone Financial Teams), wrote my dissertation on Financial Advisor Family Teams, and have consulted to some of the Elite Financial Teams in the industry. After reading this book, I have one thing to say—this is an "Elite" book!

Matt has truly provided us with a framework for building an Elite Financial Team and has done this in a unique way. I thought it would be helpful if we heard directly from the author about the book and his journey so I put together questions for Matt to respond to. Below are my questions and his responses:

RICHARD: "Matt, first of all, congratulations on this great book (or might I say "Elite" book). This book provides a clear road map for the Advisor who wants to take their business to the next level and beyond. Let's start with . . . producing a book like this is no easy task—especially while running a successful practice and family. How did you do it?"

MATT: "Writing a book is always both an adventure and a challenge. Since this is my 11th book, I've developed a formula of sorts, or at least a process that works for me. It starts with a research project, in this case we researched team for over three years, then I'll write a research report, and if there is enough material, I'll write a book. Since I travel a lot giving speeches, I spend many nights alone in hotel rooms—not exciting, but an excellent time for writing. I try to write at least something every day."

RICHARD: "Matt, you learned from your research that only 17% of the Advisors that were studied displayed Elite Team characteristics. Given your national perspective and experience with Advisors, why do you believe this is the case—in other words, what have you found to be the greatest obstacles hindering Advisors to reach this level of performance?"

MATT: "The reason only 17% of all financial teams are full-functioning, or as I refer to them in the book as "elite", is because most teams are not formed properly. Advisors hastily enter into a team arrangement without considering all the complexities of this business arrangement. Essentially, a financial team is like a business marriage. Not only do partners need to be compatible, they need to have comparable work ethic, and be in agreement on the long-range goals of the team. This involves the quality and number of support personnel, budgets, annual growth projections, and so on—it requires a lot of work, which is why it so often overlooked or assumed. Also, if a team isn't on a growth track it is likely to become dysfunctional, with partners arguing over work ethic and money—which is never healthy."

RICHARD: "With every challenge comes an opportunity—at least this is how Elite Performers tend to view life's experiences. To say the least, Advisors are in a very challenging environment given the systemic changes and dislocations that continue to occur. Given this reality, how can Advisors use this book to navigate their direction as a lighthouse provides "light" for ships in the night?"

MATT: "Yes. This is an extremely challenging environment for everyone. However, elite teams have a distinct advantage and not only will weather this financial tsunami, they will thrive. Why? Because they are the real deal, and today's affluent consumer is so skeptical—the trust factor with major financial institutions has been severely damaged, and the affluent are desperate for guidance, for help. Elite teams are perfectly to provide both the trust and guidance the affluent are desperately searching for. This book is designed to be a roadmap for any team or group of advisors thinking of forming a team—the idea is to mirror the best practices of these elite teams. It takes work, but it certainly can be done."

RICHARD: "In closing, what future research are you considering to help Advisors and Teams continue to prosper?"

MATT: "My next research project is probably going to focus on the affluent. I'm very curious to get a handle on their trust factor, their expectations, and the changes, if any, they are making as a result of this financial meltdown."

So if you want to reach the Elite level in your business and are willing to do the work, act on the methodology outlined described in this book; and if you are part of a team, have everyone on your team act upon it as well. You owe it to yourself and your clients to strive to be part of the 17% solution!

Richard Orlando, Ph.D.
Industry Teams Expert

More frequently asked questions . . .

QUESTION: Do the affluent really prefer a team over a sole practitioner?

ANSWER: Yes and no. Our research is explicit on what the affluent are looking for from a financial professional. They want comprehensive wealth management that is delivered with personalized first-class service and a high level of efficiency. Elite teams have a definite advantage, and our research tells us that it's a statistically significant advantage. However, it's important to keep in mind that only 17% of financial teams enjoy this statistical advantage. Most teams, like most solo advisors, are still trying to figure it out.

QUESTION: Can financial advisors who are not temperamentally suited to teamwork compete with financial teams?

ANSWER: Yes, but it takes an exceptional FA to do so. Why? Because it requires a radical shift in temperament. Most likely if you are of this nature you will need to build strategic alliances with experts (CPAs, JDs, bankers, insurance providers), and hire one to three support personnel to emulate the breadth of services offered by an Elite Financial Team. In other words, you'll have to become a "virtual financial team." I've seen solo practitioners do this, and you can argue that they really DO have a team. What's more, solo practitioners who follow this formula are almost ALWAYS more successful than loose confederations of advisors.

QUESTION: Is team member turnover a big deal in terms of impact on clients?

ANSWER: YES! Any form of turnover sounds an alarm. Stability provides a level of comfort for affluent clients. Red flags go up whenever I encounter a team with high turnover. Something is wrong. It's a telltale sign that I'm not encountering an elite team. It's a tip-off that there are probably many more factors contributing to client dissatisfaction.

Elite teams retain loyal team members, and consequently they do not lose clients because of occasional turnover. Re-visit the *service-loyalty-revenue nexus* outlined in chapter 5.

On the other hand, teams in the *Storming-Norming* trap are usually awash in conflict among team members, including support staff, which typically translates into client problems, inefficiencies, etc. Because there is no consistently high-level of client satisfaction, when good advisors leave, they often "steal" clients with whom they have strong relationships—albeit, never as many as they think. Why not as many? Because even if they were good advisors, the services they delivered as a team were sub-standard, and this reflects on them as individuals.

QUESTION: How often should teams meet?

ANSWER: As discussed in Chapter 8, effective teams should have both a weekly meeting, if appropriate a support personnel meeting, and a daily five-minute huddle. At the Oechsli Institute, we recommend a Team Meeting Planning Checklist, which stipulates that meetings must have a purpose, must be time-sensitive, must have an agenda, must involve *all* team members, and must end *on time*, with clear action items for everyone who's attended. Accountability is also woven through the fabric of each meeting. The leader should facilitate the weekly team meeting. He or she needn't lead the meeting, but should facilitate open, honest feedback and keep the meeting on track.

Practice managers at larger elite teams often hold weekly staff meetings that they facilitate, which include all support personnel reporting to the practice manager. These meetings are most effective when they're held within 24 hours prior to the weekly team meeting.

Daily huddles are informal chats, with everyone standing, to review the upcoming day. These work best when they have an element of structure—i.e., they take place at the same time and place every day . . . even if that's in the break room or by the water cooler.

QUESTION: How long should team meetings last?

ANSWER: Weekly team meetings should be time-specific and time-sensitive. The most effective weekly meetings last 30 to 45 minutes, and no more than an hour. In poorly led meetings, people arrive late, some blowhard talks endlessly and (therefore) the meetings never end on time. That's because there is little, if any accountability. Nobody is rushing to conclude the meeting, and nothing much is accomplished.

Contrast this with the meetings held by elite teams, where time is at a premium because people are busy, accountability is the norm, everyone participates and stays on point, and a great deal is accomplished.

Case in point: a typical meeting held by The Founder's Team. The young, attractive and incompetent assistant, and two useless junior advisors posturing as marketing experts, did not hold their team meetings on a weekly basis. But when they did hold meetings, they dragged on forever. And the junior advisors always had a hidden agenda when "facilitating" these meetings, which usually involved stirring up trouble in an attempt to appear important. Team leader Chuck allowed this to occur. He didn't know how to conduct an effective meeting, because nobody ever taught him how, and he liked the idea of "holding court" in front of his team on those occasions when he wasn't (literally) phoning in his views. Needless to say, these meetings were a waste of time.

QUESTION: Can you provide an example of a team that handled compensation fairly vs. a team that did NOT handle compensation fairly?

ANSWER: Okay, here's an example of a team that did NOT handle it properly.

I refer to this group as the "Purgatory Team." A father created a large practice, and then brought in his son and son-in-law. His objective was to turn over the business to them. He prematurely gave them MUCH too large a percentage of his business, well before they'd earned it, and made them equal majority partners. Meanwhile, the father gradually, or maybe not so gradually, semi-retired. However you slice it, the former Team Leader stopped leading the team.

The father's personal assistant was now dependent on the "boys" for her bonus, as was the team's financial planner, whom the father had hired a few years earlier. The new partners quickly became enamored of their new incomes and lifestyles (both immediately bought showcase homes in upscale neighborhoods), but—for some reason—they decided to cut the salaries of the assistant and the planner. Whether this was out of hubris, naïveté, or pure greed, they convinced themselves that because these individuals weren't directly responsible for bringing in new business, they were overpaid. Maybe so, but it's VERY dangerous to cut somebody's salary, especially since these newly knighted partners were "silver spooned" advisors who were handed a business they didn't create.

What was even more ironic, without the father's direct assistance, the son and son-in-law were incapable of bringing in new business.

Surprise! Both support personnel quit.

Naturally, this wreaked havoc within a team that was quickly becoming entrenched in the *Storming-Norming* trap. The son and son-in-law were soon forced to hire a temporary assistant and take over the financial planning responsibilities themselves until they could find another planner. Word soon spread on the "street" (business community) that these guys were "silver spoon brats" with large egos—that they were hard to work for, greedy and (also) cheap.

Because this team has a strong foundation, thanks to 30+ years of work by the father, and because it's a family team, it's destined to be stuck in Purgatory.

The following is an example of an elite team that handled compensation fairly.

This team was headed by a senior partner, and included three junior partners (advisors), a practice manager, and three additional support personnel. Each has a percentage of the practice (with the largest share going to the Team Leader), each is responsible for managing a specific number of relationships (and generating a specific amount of revenue), and each is responsible for a specific amount of Rainmaking (albeit much less than the Team Leader).

The team employs a metrics system that measures the productivity of everyone. When the team hits its targets (production, new assets, client retention, Rainmaking, etc.), which they do more often than not, there is a substantial bonus pool distributed proportionately to every member. Each team member's bonus is linked to his individual contribution to the team's goals as determined by ongoing performance reviews. This compensation system is somewhat complicated, and requires accountability and strong leadership, but it is *very* fair, and strengthens the loyalty of all team members. Not surprisingly, all of the team members usually hit their goals.

SECTION IV

Ensuring an Ongoing Focus on Growth

11

The Critical Path Method

Elite Financial Teams are far more accountable to their business plans, at every level, than other teams.

—Factoid, Financial Team Research

The Critical Path Method (CPM) was developed in the 1950s by DuPont Corporation and the Rand Corporation as a way to address the challenges of shutting down chemical plants for maintenance and then restarting them once the work was completed. Today, the CPM is commonly used with all forms of projects: construction, software development, research projects, product development, engineering, etc. This methodology essentially focuses on: 1) Identifying all activities required to complete a project, which is also known as 'work breakdown structure" (for teams this translates into breaking down the long-range business plan into annual goals and metrics, complete with individual roles, responsibilities and tasks); 2) establishing a timeline each activity will require for completion (including annual goals, quarterly metrics and individual accountability), and 3) the dependencies between the activities—i.e., the interrelated aspects of team members' roles and performance.

We've simplified this methodology to create a tool that's designed to ensure that teams stay on track toward their annual goals, which in turn are linked to their long-range business plans. The objective is to make certain that every action of every team member is linked to these objectives—in other words, on the team's "Critical Path."

Consider the following three practical disciplines of Jim Collins in the box below in terms of your team's critical path. They are direct and full of common sense. But without a critical path, it is unlikely these disciplines would be acted upon, and if they were, it would be unlikely that they would last for any length of time.

The "Level 5 Leader"

To get the right people on the bus and build a superior team, Jim Collins proposes "three practical disciplines for being rigorous rather than ruthless" in *Good to Great*:

- *"Practical Discipline #1: When in doubt, don't hire—keep looking.* Those who build great companies understand that the ultimate throttle on growth for any great company is not markets, or technology, or competition, or products.

It is one thing above all others: the ability to get and keep enough of the right people." Elite teams are very careful about adding new team members, regardless of their role.

- *"Practical Discipline #2: When you know you need to make a people change, act.* The good-to-great companies showed the following bipolar pattern at the top management level: People either stayed on the bus for a long time or got off the bus in a hurry. In other words, the good-to-great companies did not churn more, they churned better."

Elite teams recognize that the team is only as productive as its weakest link. They do not tolerate unsatisfactory performance, there are no excuses, and they make changes quickly. Meanwhile, the typical team chugs and sputters along with the "wrong people on the bus."

- *"Practical Discipline #3: Put your best people on your biggest opportunities, not your biggest problems.* There is an important corollary to this discipline: When you decide to sell off your problems, don't sell of your best people. This is one of those little secrets of change. If you create a place where the best people always have a seat on the bus, they're more likely to support changes in direction."

Because of the selectivity process, the competency, and loyalty engendered, members of elite teams are never worried about their positions. For instance, many teams struggle with inventory issues (breaking free from clients who generate little or no revenue) because team members are insecure, and they see their role attached to servicing these non-revenue producing clients. Hence these members are likely to resist (or even sabotage) efforts to jettison smaller clients.[6]

It all starts with the business plan.

Again, every Elite Financial Team has a written business plan that contains clearly defined and time-specific goals linked to the plan. For instance: one team's long-range business plan was to acquire 50 new affluent clients within the next four years that would bring their total assets under management to $1 billion. They wanted to be *the* relationship manager—*the* "go-to" financial coordinator for each of these new affluent relationships.

Their first challenge was segmenting their existing clients and jettisoning all that were under $1 million. This was a six month process. At the time, they had 300 clients and slightly less than $800 million in discretionary assets. Therefore, their annual goal was to jettison 150 households (get rid of 150 client relationships) and bring in about 12 new relationships worth $100 million. (Previously, they determined that approximately 35 of their current clients were generating 90% of their revenue, and that the 150 households they wanted to unload represented no more than $25 million in assets.)

The CPM was the way they ensured that they didn't stray from their long-range objective: $1 billion from 50 households. This meant that every activity, every role and every area of responsibility of each team member had to be linked to this objective. Because servicing those 150 households was not linked to the objective, because it would pull the entire team from their "critical path," the decision was made to "detach" those households.

---

6 Collins, Jim. *Good to Great: Why Some Companies Make the Leap and Others Don't.* New York; Harper-Collins, 2001, pp. 54-59.

Creating Your Team's *Critical Path System*

In the world of Elite Financial Teams, it's all about relationships. Every aspect of attracting, servicing and developing loyal wealthy clients involves building strong relationships with them, their centers-of-influence, individual team member's centers-of-influence, referral alliances and affluent prospects. Your *Critical Path System* must be designed to help your team's Rainmaker(s) plan her week so she can spend at least 70% of her time face-to-face with the highest priority people.

The idea behind the *Critical Path System* is to link every action to your long-range business plan and annual metrics scorecard. You want to base it on a simple principle: planning works best when it's both tactical (short term) and strategic (long-term). We've found that it's critical to plan your team's Rainmaking activities one week at a time, and make certain every team member's activities support these affluent relationship-building activities.

If you keep it simple, by focusing on affluent relationships, you can start each week by reviewing your team's *Critical Path Organizer* to determine the meetings you will schedule, materials needed and the involvement of other team members. Then you can use the *Critical Path Organizer* on a daily basis during team huddles. This allows you to track progress with key relationships and keep track of vital information you uncover at each meeting.

In the Appendix, I've included a copy of our *Critical Path Organizer*. You'll find that it segments key relationships into four categories:

Top 25 Clients

Here's where you will track your Top 25 Clients. You can create your own version (it works well on an Excel spreadsheet), but be sure to keep track of:

- Your last contact with this client and by whom.
- The outcome of that contact—i.e., what happened.
- Opportunities uncovered for introductions, upgrades, intimate client events, etc.

- Surprise and Delight information—e.g., hobbies, interests, graduations, anniversaries, birthdays, etc.
- The next action step to take with this client, and by whom.

Prospects

This worksheet helps to keep track of each prospect in your team's pipeline. Too often, we hear about prospects "falling off the radar." Your team will *never* let this happen again by keeping track of:

- Each prospect's status—warm, hot, tire-kicker, etc.
- Your last contact with this prospect, and by whom.
- The next action step to take with this prospect, and by whom.
- Any intelligence gathered on this prospect: by whom + details (Bob discovered he was selling his business within the year).
- Projected assets: $12 million was Bob's share after the sale of the business.
- Surprise and Delight information and next action step—e.g., prospect is a die-hard Red Sox fan, so send him a 2007 World Championship coffee cup.

Referral Sources

You can also think of this worksheet as your strategic alliances—CPAs, attorneys, bankers, real estate agents, human resource directors, etc. Track any individual you consider a solid referral source. These relationships need to be cultivated just like affluent client and prospect relationships. Create or customize the one in the Appendix, and use your *Critical Path Organizer* to help your team track:

- Your team's last contact with this referral source, and by whom.
- The outcome of that contact.
- The opportunities that were uncovered for introductions, referrals, Surprise and Delight, etc.—what, when, and by whom.
- The next action step to take with this referral source—when and by whom.

Personal Centers-of-Influence

This worksheet is a compilation of every personal center-of-influence among all team members. It's not unusual to have a Practice Manager or another support person with excellent contacts. Frequently, these contacts go unmonitored and untapped. But, by creating a systematic approach, they can be a fertile source for ideal prospects. Think in terms of tracking:

- The last contact with this COI, and by whom.
- The outcome of that contact.
- Opportunities that were uncovered for introductions, referrals, Surprise and Delight, etc.—what, when, and by whom.
- The next action step to take with this COI—when and by whom.

Remember, the objective of these worksheets, your team's customized *Critical Path Organizer,* is to keep everyone on track. That's why the "next action step" listed above is all-important. Whether it involves your affluent clients, ideal prospects, referral sources or centers-of-influence, this method will help your team link every action to its goals. Every activity, of every team member, will help drive the dream.

Fine-Tune Roles and Responsibilities

The Critical Path Method provides a natural framework for assessing and refining roles and responsibilities.

One objective of using the CPM is to quickly identify redundancy. Even Elite Financial Teams experience fluid situations that require clearly RE-defined roles and areas of responsibility. The more frequently the metrics scorecard is updated, the easier it becomes for individuals to stay on their critical path, and the better individual performances can be quickly measured and *compensated* accordingly. In this area, some common mistakes include:

1. Not re-visiting the established roles and responsibilities.
2. Designating clearly defined roles and responsibilities on paper, but not taking the time to create a Critical Path Method for your team.

3. Ditto #2, but not having the right people on the "bus" or in the right roles. The objective must always be to maximize each team member's core-competencies.
4. Ditto #2, but not measuring individual performance and organizing his/her compensation, bonuses, promotions, career counseling (or firing) accordingly.

Re-visit Performance Expectations and Metrics

Make certain that your Elite Financial Team stays on its critical path (which must be linked to annual goals and the long-range business plan). The key to discipline is helping a disciplined person stay disciplined. And the same goes for helping high performers meet elite expectations. They won't mind the help. It's only the non-performers who get annoyed, because you're reminding them that they're underperforming. In fact, if you're currently the leader of a dysfunctional team, which means your performance expectations are not being met and people do not appreciate you re-visiting their performance expectations, you may want to "play it back" to the Forming stage and work through the *Forming* checklist in Chapter 2.

This is an excellent exercise for any team that finds itself struggling. Play it back to the Forming stage, and assess everything! Whenever a team is stuck in the *Storming-Norming* trap, they will either experience an ugly divorce or remain stuck in purgatory, neither of which is a good result. Therefore, by starting all over—by asking "what are our objectives, why was this team formed, who is responsible for what—and by paying attention to getting the right people on the "bus" and making sure there is an accountability process for everyone, you can experience a renaissance.

Summary

- Accountability to the team's business plan is a constant theme found in elite teams.
- Creating your team's Critical Path Method (CPM) will strengthen discipline and accountability while providing your entire team with a laser focus.
- Your CPM will help you segment your key relationships into four categories: 1) top 25 clients; 2) prospects; 3) referral sources, and 4) personal centers-of-influence.
- Your CPM will also help you "get the right people on the bus." Either they stay on your critical path or they . . . are . . . outta here!
- Assessment tools can help you in the selection process, but they are not bulletproof. Most decision-making must be made by the Team Leader, senior partners and Practice Manager.
- Revisiting performance expectations and fine-tuning roles will be a natural byproduct of your team's CPM.
- If performance expectations are causing a problem because they are not being met, revisit the *Forming* checklist as an entire team.

12

Annual Team Retreat/ Quarterly Review

Elite teams are much more likely to hold quarterly reviews and annual retreats.

—*Factoid, Financial Team Research*

It's very important that teams comprehensively review their collective and individual performance quarterly, so that adjustments can be made—when necessary.

Holding review meetings outside of the office is healthy, since the change in venue sends a signal: this is important! It also facilitates more open and honest discussion, without the typical constraints that come with being in the office, which include various interruptions, phone calls, in-person meetings, etc. This is a mini-team-building exercise, where everyone can be treated to a late lunch (or early dinner), and can even enjoy a few drinks with colleagues after the review meeting.

An Annual Team Retreat should take place over the course of one to two days during the *Forming Stage*, and should be held annually thereafter. The objectives of the Annual Retreat are:

- *Team Accountability.* A performance review of the entire team regarding annual goals and linking of goals to long-range goals. This may include a Critical Path Review, linking everything to the aforementioned performance gaps.

Essentially, this is where the rubber meets the road of performance. If one of your team goals is to bring in $60 million of net new assets, the entire team needs to be accountable for that number. If the team falls short of the goal, a serious Critical Path discussion should take place that addresses all that is involved. Once again, this accountability exercise is not productive if it becomes a "blame-throwing" drill.

Recently, I was asked to assist a very successful financial team in creating an agenda for their annual retreat. They always have lofty targets, and though they are meeting a number of their annual metrics—including new affluent relationships, fee revenue and production—they missed two significant goals: their three-year discretionary asset goal (this annual retreat happened to coincide with the completion of their three-year business plan) and affluent client loyalty.

The Team Leader was committed to having $1 billion of discretionary assets under management and, even though they were planning to bring in $100 million for the year, they were going to fall short. After serious deliberation, we determined that the best course of action was to move the timeline another two quarters. This would enable everyone to remain positive. Instead of three years, it would take three years and 6 months. This would let the team reset another long-range target, and the team leader was already focused on the "next billion." His thinking was that, at times, not everyone possessed the same sense of urgency, though he couldn't complain about their overall success as a team.

Losing two wealthy clients was another matter. Their annual target is always 100% affluent client retention! We decided to address this as an overall team service and relationship-management issue. That provided the context for the team to conduct a brainstorming exercise. The irony was that they prided themselves on providing top-level service, which is why everyone's input was essential for fine-tuning their service model.

- ***Individual Accountability.*** A performance review from a team perspective: what needs to be refined, improved, etc. Using the *Performance Standards Worksheet* in the Appendix, you can combine individual accountability with an area of responsibility. In most instances, there is more than one team member involved.

It is important to review the performance standards for that particular area of responsibility, as well as the description of that area. It is also important to have clarity and standards assigned to each area. Then, you will want to break the accountability into quality, convenience, personalization and value expectations.

In the situation I mentioned above, the Team Leader was the primary person responsible for Rainmaking. Therefore, he was the team member who was most accountable for falling behind the team's three-year goal. In this instance, he accepted responsibility, and agreed with the team's assessment of "why" he got off track. Two years ago, he commissioned the construction of his dream beach home. Although he wasn't hammering the nails, it pulled him off track for nearly a year. No wonder the team fell short of their target! He resolved to never allow himself to get sidetracked again.

Only time will tell, but his beach house is complete, and he appears more driven to reach his asset projections. This, by-the-way, is also one of the reasons he is a highly effective leader of an elite team. There are many Team Leaders who would never allow themselves to be held accountable to other team members.

The loss of two wealthy clients was a more complex issue. It involved three, if not four, team members. The Team Leader failed to schmooze these two clients enough, because, by his own admission, he didn't get along with them very well. His negligence in managing these relationships trickled down to his Practice Manager and other support personnel to the extent that they were not even part of the team's Top 25 *Critical Path Organizer.* During the team retreat, corrective measures were enacted to make certain this never happened again.

- ***Critical Path Action Plan.*** This involves the upcoming year's goals, metrics, individual expectations and individual action plans. Actually, this should be an active component of every performance-based exercise you work through during the retreat. There is nothing worse than discussing an issue, especially one essential to performance, and keeping the conversation at 35,000 feet before moving to the next agenda item. Not only does this do nothing to improve performance, it often has a detrimental effect—not much different than a mother giving a lecture to her children on the importance of eating vegetables, but eating out at fast-food establishments where french-fries are considered a vegetable.

Also, these 35,000-foot discussions can easily become a platform for a team member to grandstand. Nothing turns off team members more than a colleague who constantly hogs the floor.

- ***Brainstorming.*** By focusing on one to three performance gaps the Team Leader wants to address (creatively), this exercise can tackle potential obstacles, new ventures, future opportunities, etc.

This is very similar to *project mapping*, where an issue is identified—say, "More Effective Team Meetings"—and then placed in the middle of a white board with a box drawn around it. The idea is to work from the center outward.

Next, everyone is asked to think of items that could improve team meetings. In brainstorming, every item is recorded: there is no right or wrong when it comes to brainstorming. Each item is then written on the board and connected by a line to the box in the middle. When the original flow of ideas begins to trickle down, the next step is getting everyone to help prioritize each item connected to the box.

Finally, you want to develop an *action plan* from your prioritized ideas, and agree to either file or flush the brainstorming thoughts that you've collected.

- ***Team building.*** Individual team members build trust with each other—often having each member complete some form of a behavioral assessment tool prior to the retreat as an ice-breaker for discussion. Each team member highlights a truth about herself that is described in the assessment, something that might not be obvious to others, as well as something that is "spot on," which everyone is aware of and is often humorous.

The idea is to get everyone interacting with each other outside of their professional role. This is why Outward Bound programs gained popularity. Rope courses, scaling walls, walking barefoot over hot coals and other physical activities became fashionable for demonstrating teamwork and out-of-comfort-zone courage. In these events, individuals are usually asked to be supportive of one another, and at times actually assist one another in performing the activity.

Personally, I was always suspect of the transferability of physical out-of-comfort-zone (controlled daredevil activities) with making tough decisions at work. My suspicions were put to the test when I was asked to participate in a ropes course team-building exercise following a keynote speech I delivered at a leadership conference. The conference was held at a resort in Beaver Creek, Colorado, but our ropes course required a caravan of jeeps, since the course was on a mountain top.

After everyone loaded into the jeeps, a jovial camaraderie seemed to mask the anxiety most of us felt. Other than the executive who organized this excursion, everyone was leery about what we were getting ourselves into. After what seemed like another two miles up the mountain, we stopped in a circular gravel-mud parking area that was anchored by some sort of a lodge-shelter structure.

No sooner had we disembarked from our jeeps, than each of us was handed a release form to sign. Neither the ropes course company nor the fund company sponsoring the activity would be responsible if any of us was injured or died. I didn't view this as a positive signal. Next, we were given instructions about the harnesses needed for our first event—scaling a horizontal vertical wall. After listening to the instructions, I wanted to get this over with, so I volunteered to be one of the first teams tackling the wall.

What happened next could never have been scripted. I was nearly at the top of the wall, working well with my partner on the ground (neither of us was afraid of heights). We were in reasonably good shape, but the other team was having all sorts of problems. The climber was afraid of heights and overweight, not a good combination. He was also one of the company's top producers. When he started to hyperventilate halfway up the wall, I had my partner lower me closer, as my role was to help him scale the wall. In the middle of trying to tell this panicked climber where to put his right hand, a thunder clap boomed in the near distance, immediately followed by an ominous bolt of lightening. This unexpected call from nature nearly caused our ground-based partners to drop our harness lines.

After the second round of thunder and lightening, we were ordered off the wall. In addition, those of us with metal harnesses were instructed to take them off and get as far away from them as possible. Everyone dropped whatever equipment he had, and formed little groups in an open area to wait for the storm to blow over. Nature had other ideas.

Within minutes, we were in the midst of a thunderstorm on the top of a mountain. None of us had to wait for instructions from our outfitter guides to run 200 yards uphill on a muddy path to the shelter. Drenched and exhausted, the group revolted at waiting out the storm and continuing the rope course.

Although the executive who organized this experience was well meaning, he hadn't thought about the X-factor that often accompanies such activities. He felt so guilty that he sponsored an open bar for the rest of the afternoon. As you can imagine, the team building camaraderie then took on an entirely different flavor.

The irony was that much of the bar-talk revolved around an underperformer who was a tri-athlete—not the top producer I was trying to coax up the wall. The team members were convinced that the underperformer would have excelled at every aspect of the rope course, but would continue to under-perform because his head wasn't in the game. The top producer admitted that he was never going to attempt a rope course again, but would always be one of the firm's top-quintile performers. Go figure.

Team building is an important aspect of any retreat. Whenever human beings are interacting on a consistent basis, there will always be a benefit for getting everyone involved in some activity that involves a good amount of personal interaction that isn't work related. Here are some things to keep in mind:

- *Communication.* Always striving to improve interpersonal communications, identify communication gaps, and search for ways to improve. There are numerous exercises that can facilitate communication. My rope course experience inadvertently opened up lines of communication among colleagues that had never existed before. Obviously, you don't have to experience life-threatening exercises to open up communication.

Breaking down barriers can be accomplished by simply pairing two team members who don't interact much with each other. They can work through one of the exercises I've outlined in Chapter 12. There's no magic formula for communication: it's all about being open, honest and respectful of other people's feelings. Nobody appreciates brutally honest communication.

- *Conflict Resolution.* This involves understanding individual personality styles for dealing with conflict. There are a number of ways to address this issue, and whether you care to admit it or not, conflict within a team should be expected. This is why resolving conflict is essential for any elite team.

You can address this either by working on a specific "practice case" that involves conflict, or tackling a legitimate real-life issue. Let me offer a word of caution about dealing with real conflicts: they can escalate quickly if one team member perceives that he is getting blind-sided or ganged-up on. Whenever you plan on dealing with real conflict, make certain everyone is fully aware which issue is going to be discussed, and that the ground rules will be as follows:

- All input must be constructive.
- Each team member must give input.
- Each team member must provide support for their input.
- Nothing is to be on a personal level.
- Action steps for resolution are the objective.

I always advise providing these ground rules (or some variation) as well as the issue in conflict a couple weeks in advance of the retreat. This allows everyone to give serious thought to the issue at hand.

Every serious team should devote two full days at the end of each year, the Fourth Quarter, to an off-site retreat to perform the exercises detailed in the next chapter. They should also consider shorter, half-day off-site retreats each quarter to measure progress and shore up any problems.

13

Team Retreat Exercises

Depending on the length of time most team members have spent working together, you may want to open your team retreat with either (or both) of the following exercises. They're designed to encourage team members to "open up" without fear of harsh criticism.

Ice-Breaker Exercise #1

The "4" Facts

Objective: This golden oldie is easy to facilitate. It's designed to open communications between team members and deepen the understanding of each individual. Everyone will learn more about her teammates while also strengthening team camaraderie.

Time Required: 20 to 30 minutes

Instructions:
Each team member writes out four personal facts, but only three of them are true. In order to discover the single *untruth*, everyone must listen closely, which increases interest in the exercise. A competitive element can be added by offering a prize to the person who guesses the most correct answers.

- All team members write down four facts about themselves; three that are true (things others don't know) and one that is false.
- Then one at a time, each team member will read their four facts to the team.
- The other team members are challenged to guess which "fact" is the lie.

Ice-Breaker Exercise #2

"Favorite Relative"

Time Required: 10 to 15 minutes

Objective: Another golden oldie, this is designed to be non-threatening, but still reveal a little about each team member's extended family, personal values, and how they've been influenced during their formative years.

Instructions:

- Each team member selects her favorite relative—a grandparent, aunt, uncle or cousin.
- Then she must identify two qualities that made the person special.
- Each team member then shares her "favorite relative" and the two qualities with the rest of the group.

Strengthening Trust

Now that we've broken the ice, it's time to get down to the nitty gritty exercises, starting with:

Peeling Back the Onion

Objective: To deepen the level of understanding of each individual team member in a non-threatening way and allow each individual a safe venue for revealing more of their personal self.

Time required: Approximately 20 minutes, depending upon the size of the team, 3-5 minutes per team member.

Instructions:
A. Have everyone discuss the following two topics:

- How many brother and sisters they have and where each team members falls within the sibling hierarchy.
- A special and memorable event in their childhoods.

Note: You can vary these topics in many ways with discussions about favorite foods, last book read, second favorite hobby, and so on. But it's important to keep these discussion points non-threatening. For instance you don't want to ask "What is the biggest challenge you've had with one of your children?"

B. After everyone has participated in discussing the topics you have selected, facilitate a discussion about what the team members discovered about each other. This is designed to strengthen communication through a deeper understanding of your team members. This exercise is fun, revealing, and builds trust.

Strengthening Communication

Behavioral Style

Objective: To improve communication among team members by gaining a better understanding of their behavioral style. This will include to the dos and don'ts of communication as they relate to each team member.

Time required: About an hour, depending on the size of your team.

Instructions:
Every team member must have completed a recent behavior assessment within two weeks of the off-site meeting, and have brought their personal profiles along with them. From the personal profile, all team members should:

- Share two dos and two don'ts for communicating with them.
- A discussion should follow on what changes, if any, should be made to improve communication with the different team members. This should be fun, light-hearted, but also useful.
- Each team member then shares an area highlighted in his profile that he would like to improve.
- A discussion should follow with constructive feedback from other team members.
- Each team member than shares something he disagrees with concerning his personal profile assessment
- A discussion should follow—again, light and fun.

Note: You can use these personal profile assessments in many different ways. But be sure there is no "right" and "wrong" profile. This exercise, though personal and insightful, needs to be fun and helpful. If a team member becomes defensive, move on to another person.

After everyone has participated, discuss what you have learned about yourself and your teammates, and what you will strive to change.

Conflict Resolution

Overcoming Tough Issues

Objective: Develop a positive framework for handling conflict within the team.

Time required: This depends upon the tough issue to be resolved, but no longer than 90 minutes. This issue must NOT be of a personal nature—e.g., a disagreement over an individual team member's work ethic.

Instructions:
You can select any tough issue, as long as it's not personal. It could be bandwidth (number of clients), office location, interior decoration, technology upgrade, collateral material, adding another team member, etc.

The key is framing the tough issue, one that often leads to conflict, in a manner that encourages—or at least allows—for disagreement, and that steers the group toward a resolution in a professional and non-threatening manner.

- One individual identifies and frames a tough issue, such as raising the account minimum versus staying with the status-quo.
- One team member should be the designated scribe for the exercise, and categorize comments on a white board as either **Positive** or **Negative**.
- Each team member will write down individual preferences, along with her supporting arguments.
- Each team member then shares her preference and supporting arguments, while everyone else listens and asks relevant questions.
- The scribe documents the key points under the appropriate headings of positive or negative.
- A team discussion follows to discuss preferences, the pros and cons and, if necessary, the Team Leader facilitates a final resolution.

Performance Enhancer

Heroes

Objective: Raising the bar. This is a powerful and motivational exercise I've been using in workshops for over 25 years. It always gets people thinking about achievement from a different perspective. The idea is that everyone selects a hero from history or a real-life role model, and lists the qualities and characteristics that make the hero special. Almost magically, everyone begins focusing on higher levels of achievement.

The objective is actually twofold: first, associate every team member with a personal hero, and second, to force everyone to really think about the qualities –internal qualities (IQs) and school-taught qualities (SQs) that made (or make) this individual special.

In my experience, team members classify 90% to 100% of the important "hero qualities" as IQ—those not taught in school, even though our society places the most emphasis on SQ.

Time Required: 30 to 45 minutes

Instructions:

- Each team member writes down the name of a hero from history, or a real-life role model
- Then each person lists the qualities and characteristics that make this individual special to her.
- After everyone has selected a hero or role model, and exhausted the list of qualities and characteristics, she now has to label the hero as either IQ (inner qualities that have been learned through the lessons of life, role modeling, etc.), or SQ (school qualities that have been taught in a classroom, tested, and graded).
- Each team member names her hero / role model, lists 5 key qualities, and calculates the ratio between the IQ and SQ qualities.

Replicating Achievements

The Achievement Cycle

Objective: To foster the concept of achievement, and reinforce the concept that everyone, in his own way, is capable of being a high achiever throughout his life.

Time Required: 45 to 60 minutes

Instructions:

The idea is that everyone should recognize an achievement in his past, the sacrifices he made, how he ventured outside his comfort zone, how proud he is of his accomplishment, as well as how he feels about replicating that entire achievement cycle.

It's important to frame this in a way that shows that achievement patterns are instinctive, and that no one achievement is better than another, since this MUST NOT become an ego contest of who has the biggest achievement. To set the tone, I recommend that the Team Leader go first, sharing a meaningful accomplishment that does not come across as braggadocio.

- Everyone writes down a major accomplishment from his past—a serious goal that was achieved.
- The team member re-visits how he made it happen, his pattern of achievement, his thought process that led to the achievement, his actions, how far outside his comfort zone he ventured to accomplish the goal, etc.
- Everyone shares his achievement and re-visits what was required to achieve the goal.

The Team Leader wraps it up by explaining that achievement patterns are instinctive, as long as we challenge ourselves. Setting personal and professional goals, and then disciplining ourselves to do what is required, even if we are uncomfortable, is what is required. Everyone has done this before: let's do it again.

Commitment Confirmation

Verifying Collective Commitment

Objective: Essentially, this is a wrap-up to be conducted by the Team Leader or a facilitator. The idea is to ensure that each segment of the off-site meeting is clear and universal agreement is reached.

Time required: Five to ten minutes.

Instructions:

- At the end of the segment, the Team Leader or facilitator asks the team what has been agreed upon regarding each exercise.
- Each team member must participate.
- If there is confusion, further discussion must occur to eliminate any confusion. All commitments must be clear and agreed upon by the entire group.
- The Team Leader or facilitator should record each commitment on the white board.
- Every individual should also record the commitments.

Annual Retreat / Off-Site

PRE-WORK

1. Complete the Oechsli Institute (OI) benchmarking software assessment (benchmarking your team against the statistical best practices).
    - Three weeks prior to off-site
2. Review the OI benchmarking report, and discuss the performance gaps uncovered with your practice manager and senior partners.
    - Two weeks prior to off-site
3. Each team member completes her personal behavioral profile assessment.
    - Two weeks prior to off-site
4. Each team member identifies a professional and personal goal she will commit to achieving during the upcoming year—complete with action plan. This should be so simple that each goal and action plan can be written on the back of a business envelope.
    - Assigned two weeks prior to off-site
5. The Team Leader creates an agenda for the off-site, using gaps identified in the benchmarking assessment, annual accomplishments in relationship to the team's business plan, etc.
    - Two weeks prior to off-site
6. The Team Leader verifies the attendance of all members (attendance should be mandatory), and provides logistics (time, location, etc.).
    - Two weeks prior to off-site
7. The Team Leaders reminds all team members to bring their personal behavioral profiles, and personal and professional "back-of-envelope" goals and action plans.
    - Two days prior to off-site

Annual Retreat / Off-Site: Sample Agenda

Day One:

AM

1. **Overview of Retreat Agenda**—Team Leader; 10 minutes
2. **State of the Team Address**—Team Leader's overview of team's annual performance. This should serve as the platform for the entire off-site; 45 to 60 minutes
3. **Team Benchmark Gap Assessment**—Team Leader or facilitator led. This is a lengthy and important exercise. Action items will surface and should be combined with insights from the State-of-the-Team address; Two to three hours. You might consider a break in the middle of this exercise.
4. **Action Items**—discussion of assignments of responsibility for each action item that surfaced from the Team Benchmark Gap Assessment. This is a continuation of Benchmark Gap Assessment. This could easily become an open and lengthy discussion. If so, it should be continued at a later stage during the off-site; One hour or less.
5. **Commitment Verification**—as outlined above; Five to ten minutes.

Lunch

PM

1. **Strengthening Trust**—use Peeling-Back-The-Onion exercise, or something similar, as it's a good way to start after lunch; 20 minutes.
2. **Strengthening Communication**—Behavioral Profile exercise. This should be both informative and fun; One hour.
3. **Personal & Professional Goals**—individual goal pre-work to be shared and discussed. The objective is to make certain everyone is growing, all goals are in harmony with team goals, and there is team member support; One hour.
4. **Team Goal Discussion**—upcoming annual expectations, both

as a team and individuals. Team goals must be measurable, realistic, yet big enough to ensure growth. Every team member must be committed, and their professional goals should be linked to the growth of the team. Strengths and weaknesses and upcoming expectations; Two hours.

5. **Commitment Verification**—as outlined about; Five to ten minutes.

Day Two:

AM

1. **Re-cap of off-site**—Team Leader to discuss the highlights of day one and reinforce the commitments; 20 minutes.
2. **Individual Roles and Responsibilities**—each team member is to discuss what is working well in his area, and identify two areas that can be improved; 45 to 60 minutes.
3. **Team discussion on Rainmaking**—Team Leader and junior Rainmakers discuss what is working and what can be improved; 45 to 60 minutes.
4. **Team discussion on Practice Management**—practice manager and support personnel discuss what is working and what they want to improve; 45 to 60 minutes.
5. **Commitment Verification**—as outlined above, five to ten minutes.

Lunch

PM

1. **Team Leader Discussion**—led by the practice manager or another senior partner, a discussion on what is working and what can be improved; 45 to 60 minutes.
2. **Team discussion on Wealth Management Process**—team to discuss the profile of their affluent clients, the services and solutions they are currently delivering, and discuss what, if any other, services they might provide. The objective is to have an affluent client-centric process; 45 to 60 minutes.

3. **Team's 12 month Critical Path**—this is transferring team goals, individual roles, responsibilities, and expectations into a weekly and daily accountability form; 45—60 minutes.
4. **Open Team Discussion**—led by someone other than the Team Leader, to brainstorm and talk about anything that team members would like to discuss; 30 minutes.
5. **Re-cap and Complete Team Commitment Verification**—as outlined about, 15 minutes.

Off-Site Follow-up—two to three weeks after the annual retreat

- On-Site Team Meeting—to create a forum for feedback from team, to review commitments, and make certain accountability remains strong throughout the team; 60 minutes.

14

12 Commandments* for Elite Financial Teams

1. Properly Formed

This stage, *Forming*, is not only the most important of Dr. Tuckman's four stages of team development, it is also the most frequently overlooked. Tremendous time and energy is required to be effective in the *Forming* stage. This due-diligence most always (nothing is guaranteed) pays off. However, it takes work on the part of everyone involved, especially the senior partners. It's almost as though you need a "devils advocate" who will ask the hard questions and get the necessary clarification regarding individual expectations—now and in the future.

Whenever a team finds itself stuck in the *Storming-Norming* trap, it would be very medicinal to revisit this first commandment—the *Forming* stage.

2. Effective Team Leadership

Our research has identified effective Team Leadership as the most important component of an elite team. It is the Team Leader who will effectively guide the team through the stages of development, prevent the team from getting mired in the *Storming-Norming* trap, and inspire and direct it to higher levels of performance.

It is the Team Leader the will instill the accountability that ensures all 15 *Performance Factors* are operating efficiently. Without an effective

* Baker's Dozen

Team Leader, there will be no effective team meetings, and no quarterly reviews or annual retreats –no ongoing growth.

An effective leader is needed to hold team members accountable for meeting their performance expectations. A Team Leader resolves personnel issues before conflict can develop, and will make the hard decisions when necessary. A good Team Leader will never remain loyal to a non-performing team member.

Also, let's not overlook the importance of a Team Leader's role in business development. In elite teams, Team Leaders are the primary Rainmakers, and this ensures the growth of the team. It is not unusual for a Team Leader to mentor a junior partner in the art of Rainmaking.

3. Getting Good People

As I've duly noted, it's important to get the right people "on the bus." Whatever assessment tool you use to help, remember that no tool is bulletproof. At best, it will help you with about 30% of what you need to know. The rest is up to you. You must be able to determine that each team member has the proper work ethic, that each individual possesses total integrity along with the necessary skill set for the role. And that's not all: everyone must possess a positive-supportive-helpful attitude. But wait, there's still more! Each individual must be committed to the team's annual metrics (goals) and long-range business plan. Every team member has to be committed to the overall success, as you define success, of the team.

4. Written Business Plan and Metrics Scorecard

Great teams have both: annual metrics (which are essentially very specific annual goals) and a long-range business plan that they have committed to writing. These teams operate from a plan. They take their vision, which can easily become a 35,000-foot dream list, and transform it into a working game plan. This creates the context for the team. It is from this platform that a critical path can be developed.

These written business plans also serve as a tangible to which each team member can, and must, attach personal goals. Everything must be linked.

The Metrics Scorecard is simply a fancy term for annual goals, but the real issue is that these annual targets are directly linked to your team's business plan—hence, the term "scorecard."

5. Providing Comprehensive Wealth Management

The affluent want a solutions provider for the multi-dimensional aspects of their family's financial affairs. Period! Therefore Elite Financial Teams provide what the affluent want. This means your team must be fully immersed in comprehensive wealth management. And yes, these services must be delivered consistently at the highest level of professionalism. This commandment should be considered a basic requirement for any team trying to be the "real deal."

There is a tendency for teams to focus on the Team Leader's areas of strength, such as money management or financial planning, and not go much further regarding the services they offer. With today's affluent, this is a mistake. Regardless of the level of expertise you might have in these areas, or any area, of strength, this limited focus will leave your team's affluent clients vulnerable to another financial team that delivers the *full array* of wealth management services.

What makes this even more appealing is that comprehensive wealth management is one of those true "win-wins." By creating and executing a process for consistently providing comprehensive wealth management, you will ensure that your team fully monetizes the value of every affluent client.

6. First-Class Practice Management

There can be no mistaking the benchmark your affluent clients use for service. It's Ritz Carlton-quality service all the way. This level of service will always serve you well in dealing with the affluent. Similarly, their standard for operational efficiency is FedEx. This level of efficiency will always leave you in good standing with your affluent clients.

Developing two distinct levels of service (Platinum and Gold) will strengthen your ability to provide a higher level of service, as well as a more consistent level of service, to every client. All of which is essential to first-class Practice Management.

7. Obsessive Client Loyalty

Loyal clients are your acre of diamonds. The more affluent your client, the more likely it is that you can penetrate his centers-of-influence—provided someone on your team has Rainmaking skills. As our *service-loyalty-revenue nexus* illustrates, affluent loyalty is extremely profitable. This is why client loyalty must be an obsession of every team member. Every individual on the team must have his or her antenna extended for personal information that can be used to strengthen loyalty.

Surprise and delight opportunities, intimate client events and socializing are all part of the process, assuming you have mastered Commandments 5 and 6. According to one of our recent research reports, 79% of the affluent want you to care more about them as people than you do their investments. Affluent clients want you and your team to understand them, to know everything about them, and to be involved with them. This has to be a total team effort.

8. Clear Performance Guidelines

The best teams always inspect what they expect at every level, which means that every team member, including the Team Leader, all senior partners, and the Practice Manager, are scrutinizing everything. These guidelines are what enable the Practice Manager and Team Leader to conduct effective performance reviews.

Clarity in performance guidelines establishes the standards for a team. These standards become deep-rooted and serve to frame the expectations at every level, with every task and of every individual. This provides the framework for total accountability. If at some point a team member either will not, or cannot perform up to expectations, a career discussion is in order.

9. Ongoing Business Development

All elite teams are in a perpetual state of growth. Growth is their primary focus. They understand that if a team is not growing, it is dying a little bit every day. Dr. Tuckman's model for team development clearly outlines the stages of development and the danger of stagnation. Our research tells us that whenever a team stops growing, they will eventually find themselves back in the *Storming* stage.

10. 360-Degree Accountability

Think in terms of "surround-sound" accountability. Your team is accountable for delivering on all promises to your clients, and delivering with Ritz Carlton-quality service and FedEx efficiency. Each team member is accountable to his colleagues for delivering on all promises (expectations) regarding his area of responsibility. This also means that each team member is expected to pitch in whenever necessary, and accomplish whatever the task might be—at the highest level of professionalism.

360-degree accountability requires that everyone (at all times) remains accountable to the team's Long-Range Business Plan and Metrics Scorecard. This Commandment is another example of the value of the Critical Path Method (CPM).

11. Embracing of Kaizen

Ongoing improvement is the DNA of every Elite Financial Team. It is not a complicated concept, but it's much easier to talk about than to execute. Life is not stagnant, and neither are elite teams. Each component of our team model—business development, client loyalty, wealth management, practice management and Team Leadership—must be judged by the Kaizen standard of ongoing improvement.

Lodged deep within this 11th Commandment is the assurance that your team will never become complacent at any level. Top teams are consistently challenging themselves to get better. The best teams are always raising the bar.

12. Annual Team Performance Assessment

Much more so than the average team, elite teams are extremely hard on themselves. They do not tolerate excuses. There is no rationalizing mediocrity—a classic mistake of the common team. Within top teams, individual performance is never taken for granted, and neither is the collective performance of the team.

In-depth annual reviews, both for the team and each individual, are like an annual physical or a visit to the dentist. Just as there is a tendency to skip this annual visit –whether it's because you assume you are healthy or your teeth are fine, or you are in a state of denial—a team that avoids this 12th Commandment is signaling the Team Leadership that it needs attention. There can be no excuses for skipping your annual team performance assessment.

Elite teams recognize the importance of, and make the time for, these annual assessments. This is the basis for the annual team retreat. Every team member participates, annual metrics are reviewed, and necessary adjustments are made.

13. Loyal Team Members

People like being associated with a winner. Elite Financial Teams are the big winners with affluent centers-of-influence. It should come as no surprise that as each of the previous 12 Commandments outlines, elite teams engender loyal team members. Everyone is held to a higher standard, and whenever this occurs, people feel good about themselves and their jobs. A natural esprit-de-corps develops.

Elite team members are committed to working hard and smart, doing whatever is required to get the job done well. Loyal team members acquire emotional ownership in the team. They buy-in to the team's success, and do not tolerate anything less from any other team member. As George C. Scott said in the opening monologue of *Patton*, "Americans love a winner, and will note tolerate a loser!" If you substitute the words "affluent client" for "Americans," then that speech sums up the premise of this book.

Appendix

Team Forming Assessment

Instructions

This assessment is designed to help you determine whether or not you are ready to come together as a team. Each prospective team member, especially potential partners, should complete this checklist independently. It is important to respond to each statement honestly.

Scoring: Strongly Agree—4 Mildly Agree—3
Mildly Disagree—2 Strongly Disagree—1

Circle One

1. Trust

You need a 360-degree circle of trust; you must have complete trust in your partner(s) and they must have complete trust in you. This is the integrity component essential to the long-term success of a team.

I have complete trust in my potential team member(s). 1 2 3 4

2. Compatibility

Although trust is essential, you also must be able to get along in a high-pressure business environment. This is much different than enjoying each other's company socially.

We can work well together and be supportive of one another. 1 2 3 4

3. Work Ethic

Even if you trust one another and are compatible, work ethic has to be aligned among the partners. Whenever one partner perceives that he or she is working harder than the other, resentment surfaces that will ultimately lead to conflict. This will destroy a team. Everyone agree on the desired work ethic prior to forming.

I have total respect for my potential team member(s) current work ethic and fully expect that work ethic to continue as a team member—this includes scheduled vacations and personal time. 1 2 3 4

4. Competency

This should go without saying, but all team members must be fully capable of performing well in their areas of expertise. History is a fairly good indicator. For instance, if a partner has acquired very few clients over the past 12 months, he or she will probably struggle in marketing the team: aka, Rainmaking.

I have complete confidence in my potential team member(s) ability to perform their duties with complete professionalism and competence. 1 2 3 4

5. Comprehensive Business Plan

Each partner must agree on the vision of the team, the long-range goals, ideal client, number of ideal clients, assets, revenue, services to be provided, etc. This is essential for creating a "critical path" that the team will follow as it grows.

All potential team member(s) have a complete understanding of the team's projected long-range business plan, goals, and services offered—and are in complete agreement. 1 2 3 4

6. Clear & Unified Goals

Each partner has to buy-in to annual team goals, which means they must subjugate their personal goals to the collective goals.

I am willing to subjugate my personal goals to the collective goals of the team, and my potential team member(s) are willing to do the same. 1 2 3 4

7. Clear Roles & Responsibilities

Every team member should have a clear role and delegated areas of responsibility prior to forming.

I have a thorough understanding of each potential team member's role and delegated areas of responsibility. 1 2 3 4

8. Partner Contribution Clarity

Each partner should have a clear understanding of his/her individual contribution to the team's annual goals. Procedures should be in place for making partner compensation adjustments if one partner . . . —Exceeds Individual Contribution Targets, or -Falls Behind Individual Contribution Targets.

I have come to an agreement with my potential teammate(s) on my expected contribution and agree with the corresponding compensation adjustments for exceeding or falling behind my contribution targets. 1 2 3 4

9. Client Segmentation

Partners must agree before forming a team on how they will segment their current client base. Whether it is "A" and "B" or Platinum and Gold clients, they should mirror each other and agree on the appropriate levels of service to be delivered to each segment.

We have agreed on how to segment our current clients into a team "A" and "B" or Platinum and Gold clients, to ensure that all clients of a specific profile receive the same services. 1 2 3 4

10. Wealth Management Services Provided

Partners should agree on a client-centric process that is consistent for every client of a certain profile, i.e., "Platinum" versus "Gold" clients. Otherwise, you run the risk of letting each partner handle clients differently, which creates challenges in Practice Management.

We have agreed on a service model that will enable us to deliver a consistent client experience to our top and middle tier (platinum and gold) clients. 1 2 3 4

11. Compensation
A bonus structure for non-partner team members (support personnel) should be agreed on in advance. This should be based on team growth and individual contributions.

We have agreed on an annual merit-based bonus structure for all support personnel. 1 2 3 4

12. Individual Performance Reviews
You need agreement on who will conduct these, how they will be conducted, and when performance reviews of support personnel will occur.

We have agreed on a scheduled review process, complete with who will be conducting each review. Every team member will have a review conducted at least annually. 1 2 3 4

13. Basic Team Operations
You need agreement on weekly team meetings, phone coverage, office hours, etc.

We have clear team procedures for phone coverage, office hours, and weekly team meetings that are agreed upon by each prospective team member. 1 2 3 4

14. Partner Performance Reviews
Team partners must be held to the same level of accountability to perform, if not greater, as the team's support personnel. Senior partners should review junior partner, equal partners must review each other, and senior partners must allow their performance to be reviewed by junior partners.

We have agreed on a scheduled partner review process that will instill an equal level of accountability to all partners. 1 2 3 4

15. Team Performance Reviews

An annual team retreat, or similar type of off-site meeting, that is attended by every team member must be held to review past year achievements, reinforce team accountability for achieving goals, making necessary adjustments, and agreeing upon the upcoming year's team goals.

We have discussed and agreed upon on when, where, and how we will conduct our annual team performance review. 1 2 3 4

Understanding the Results

Score Breakdown

60	Perfect! What are you waiting for? Form and get on the road the high-performance.
59–54	You're ready to form, but re-visit the handful of areas that you moderately agree upon to get more clarity.
53–46	You probably think you're ready to form, but you should slow down and have a serious discussion on every area that you do not strongly agree on. I recognize this is work, but it will pay off by accelerating your team's journey to high-performance.
45–36	You aren't ready! You have a lot of work in front of you before forming as a team. Invest the time and energy now and you will know whether or not you should form a team.
< 36	Don't even think about it—you're not ready.

It doesn't take long to realize that, done properly, this forming stage requires a lot of work, which is why some steps above are frequently skipped. This is a mistake that you must be careful to avoid.

Your Total Score: ____________

Performance Standards Worksheet

No one relishes the idea of having performance standards imposed on them. At the same time, most will agree that it's important to deliver the type and level of performance that your clients demand and expect. We call those client expectations *performance results.* Here are the minimum performance results your high net worth clients will expect:

1. In terms of ***quality***:
   - Everything is done right the first time.
   - Everything is clear and understandable to the client.
   - Clients always receive knowledgeable and helpful assistance from your Team.
2. In terms of ***convenience***:
   - Everything is delivered when and where the client needs it.
   - Your Team always keeps promises made to clients.
3. In terms of ***personalization:***
   - Everything is customized to each client's unique needs and wants.
   - You continually find helpful new ways to serve each client's particular needs.
4. In terms of ***value:***
   - Clients perceive that the value you provide justifies the fees that they pay you.
   - Your value-added services are continually reducing each client's "cost" in terms of time, effort, and dollars.

By creating standards of performance for activities that impact these expectations, you significantly increase the probability that those expectations will be met.

As your team develops, you may discover other areas where things fall through the cracks, causing you to want to cover up mistakes and hope that the client involved won't be too upset. When that happens, stop and take inventory of that area using the *quality, convenience, per-*

sonalization, and *value* criteria described above. Then use the following worksheet to create the performance standards you need to prevent those problems from occurring in the future

Area: ______________________________

Description: ______________________________

____

____

Performance Standards to meet QUALITY Expectations:

____

____

____

Performance Standards to meet CONVENIENCE Expectations:

____

____

____

Performance Standards to meet PERSONALIZATION Expectations:

____

____

____

Performance Standards to meet VALUE Expectations:

____

____

____

Monitor Compliance Standards Guideline

1. Compliance monitoring should include at least the following:
   - Ongoing analysis to ensure that the team stays in compliance with SEC, state, DOL, CFTC regulations, and firm policies.
   - Establishment of *Compliance Procedures* that reduce the team's risk of enforcement actions, penalties, and negative publicity.
   - Development of forms and reports that enable you to document how the team meets obligations to regulatory authorities and to clients.
   - Make certain the team has a signed *Investment Policy Statement* for each client.
   - Periodic reviews of accounts to check for investment suitability, excessive trading and turnover, and mutual fund breakpoint violations. Accounts should reflect the goals and status of individuals in similar circumstances. High-risk strategies should be consistent with the client's signed *Investment Policy Statement.*
   - Correcting problems can help avoid client complaints and legal problems in the future.

2. Be certain to include at least the following in your Practice Manual:
   - Pertinent SEC, state, DOL, and CFTC regulations plus firm policies.
   - Your team's *Compliance Procedures.*
   - Copies of any forms and reports your team has agreed to use—with adequate instructions on how to use them.

Create Master Schedules Guideline

Some team members will do a great job scheduling appointments, activities, and events in their personal paper and pencil or electronic day planner. Others, of course, will not. The purpose behind creating master schedules is to counterbalance the impact of this reality and make certain that everyone is fully aware of time-driven activities and events.

To accomplish that, your ***Team Master Schedule*** should include the following:

- **Office hours.** Establish "normal" office hours and note them on your *Team Master Schedule.* Then post any deviations on the specific days involved.
- **Out-Of-The-Office Times.** As the team's Practice Manager, you should know when team members will be out of the office for everything from appointments to vacations. Post this information for everyone to see.
- **Client Reviews.** Quarterly, yearly, and milestone client review meetings for every client should be posted.
- **Client Events.** Client seminars, appreciation events, and any other type of scheduled client event should be posted.
- **Team Meetings and Activities.** Every meeting and activity that involves two or more team members should be posted.
- **Individual Team Member Appointments.** It would benefit everyone if you could include individual appointments, but team members will first have to reach a high level of trust and be convinced there is true value in doing so.

Even though the above may seem obvious, there is a reason for listing and describing each *Team Master Schedule* item. Complexity is the name of the master schedule game! The challenge is to find a way to easily **post these items and make them immediately available to everyone.**

Suggested Meeting Format

A consistent format provides a "no surprises" element that enables people to jump right in and go to work without having to first figure out what's going on. You can be creative about a lot of things, but the meeting format should not be on that list. Armed with a list of objectives and an agenda that everyone has already received, the person leading the meeting should do the following:

1. State the meeting objectives, and review the agenda.
2. Assign someone as Recorder . . . to record the decisions made by the team. Complete minutes are not necessary; but you must have a record of team decisions.
3. Move through the agenda items.
4. Review the decisions made, making certain the Recorder has them written correctly. Then ask the Recorder to type and distribute those decisions.
5. Determine actions to be taken, make assignments, and ask for everyone's thoughts abut the objectives and agenda items for the next meeting. Don't overlook this step!
6. Evaluate the meeting. Ask what went well, and what improvements are needed. Determine specific actions to take to improve the next meeting.

Team Meeting Planning Checklist

- Meeting OBJECTIVE(S):

  ____

  ____

  ____

- WHO should attend: ___ The entire Team

  ___ The following Team members:

  ____

  ____

  ____

- Location: ______________________________________

  Date: ____________________ Time: ____________________

- Equipment & Materials needed:

  ___ Flipchart(s) ___ Flipchart pads ___ Markers

  Other: ____

- Meeting objective(s) and agenda—complete by: ____________

  Distributed on ____________________________________

- Table set-up:

  ___ Round (*best for effective teamwork*)

  ___ U-Shaped (*when round tables are not available*)

  ___ No tables (*when you want to accelerate the time*)

- Notes:

  ____

  ____

Team Meeting Evaluation Form

Scale: 4 = Very Well 3 = Well 2 = Fair 1 = Poor

How well did we:

Clarify our meeting objectives?	4	3	2	1
Assign and use the Recorder?	4	3	2	1
Review the agenda?	4	3	2	1
Work through the agenda items?	4	3	2	1
Achieve our meeting objectives?	4	3	2	1
Utilize the knowledge of Team members?	4	3	2	1
Reach consensus decisions?	4	3	2	1
Trust and level with each other?	4	3	2	1
Actively involve ourselves in the meeting?	4	3	2	1
Set objectives/suggest agenda items for next time?	4	3	2	1

What **worked well** in this meeting?

____

____

____

What **improvements** should we make for the next meeting?

____

____

____

Streamlining Procedures Checklist

Utilize the following process whenever you discover procedures within your financial team that need to be streamlined.

1. Team member(s) responsible are to describe the procedure and the objective that it's designed to achieve.
2. Team member(s) list the procedure steps in sequence, noting who is responsible for each step.
3. Practice Manager or Team Leader works with team member(s) to evaluate the procedure as follows:

☐ Eliminate Duplication. Are tasks being performed by two different team members, or at different times in the procedure? A common inefficiency is for the same information to be gathered or generated by different people at different times.

☐ Combine Tasks. Here, you want to look for opportunities to take two different tasks and combine them, having one team member perform them as a single task.

☐ Simplify a Task. This is an ongoing challenge in my office. If we're not careful, things get more complicated than necessary. You want to discuss how each task is performed. If it sounds confusing, it is. Help the individual responsible for that task find ways to simplify it, which will reduce the time required to perform it.

☐ Eliminate a Task. Be on the lookout for opportunities to eliminate one or more tasks that do not add value to the procedure. Frankly, this is where our office is most guilty. Because we have so many things going on at the same time, we are always on the lookout for "busy work." Get rid of busy work!

☐ Eliminate "White Space." Look for paperwork that sits in someone's in-basket, waiting for attention. Establish a protocol for staying on top of your paper-flow.

- ☐ Checklists. Whenever you can create a checklist for a task, you've created leverage. Other people can perform the task, and will reduce time and errors.
- ☐ Errors. Whenever there is any ongoing mistake that has not been eliminated, or things are being overlooked, the Practice Manager should determine what is causing the error, and come up with ways to eliminate the cause.

4. Practice Manager and/or Team Leader then list the revised procedure steps and assigns responsibility for each.
5. Practice Manager and/or Team Leader reviews progress in 30 days.

Common Time Wasters

1. Go through the list of *Common Time Wasters* below. Discuss them and check all that you experience. Check an item even if only 1 person on your team experiences it. Write the name(s) of the individual(s) who experience each one. Ignore the "Control" column for now.

	Common Time Wasters	Who Experiences It	Control
	Interruptions—telephone on in person		
	Meetings that are poorly planned and led		
	Assigned a task, but not sure *what* to do		
	Assigned a task, but don't know *how* to do it		
	Unsure about priorities—everything is a crisis		
	Attempting to do too much—unrealistic time estimates		
	Having trouble saying "no"		
	Indecision and procrastination		
	Cluttered desk—personal disorganization		
	Failing to plan and organize your day		
	Trying to support/help someone who is disorganized		
	Conflict—causing a communication breakdown		
	Lack of self-discipline		
	Feeling tired		

2. Add other Time Wasters below that you experience individually, or as a Team. Note also who experiences it. Again, ignore the "Control" column for now.

Other Time Wasters	Who Experiences It	Control

3. Go through both lists on the previous tables. For each Time Waster listed, indicate whether the individual(s) have control/influence over it, using the following criteria:
   - **Control**—They are able to correct this Time Waster on their own.
   - **Influence**—They need the cooperation of others to correct this Time Waster, and they feel they can exert enough influence to correct it.
   - **None**—Not only are they unable to correct this Time Waster on their own, they have no way to influence the situation.

4. Ask each team member to use the "Personal Time Wasters" worksheet on the next page to determine how they will **eliminate the Time Wasters they can control or influence.** Complete the worksheet yourself. Start with the ones you can control, followed by the ones you can influence. For now, simply ignore the ones marked "None" on the previous worksheet page.
5. Ask each Team member to commit to eliminating Time Wasters they can *control* within ____ days and ones they can *influence* within ____ days. *(Decide how many days.)*
6. Agree to meet again in 30 days to discuss your progress. Review and celebrate each team member's progress with eliminating the Time Wasters they could control and influence. Challenge them

Time Wasters	Why It Occurs	How I Will Eliminate It

about any progress not yet made. Then discuss Time Wasters you originally marked "None" and determine together whether you can move any up to the Influence or even Control categories. If so, add them to the list to be overcome within the next ____ days. *(Set a time)*

Critical Path Organizer

This is a sample page from our Critical Path Organizer system. Use this to create custom worksheets for your Clients, Prospects, Centers-of-Influence and Referral Sources.

TOP 25 CLIENTS			
Rank	Client ▾	Last Contrast ▾	Outcome ▾
1			
2			
3			
4			
5			
6			
7			
8			
9			
10			
11			
12			
13			
14			
15			
16			
17			
18			
19			
20			
21			
22			
23			
24			
25			

Opportunity ▾	Surprise & Delight ▾	Action Steps ▾

Data Points

WEALTH MANAGEMENT TEAM PERFORMANCE
BY STAGE OF TEAM DEVELOPMENT
%17 of Elite
Financial Teams
Deviation from Average
140%
120%
100%
80%
60%
40%
20%
0%
-20%
-40%
-60%
-80%
Forming
Storming
Norming
Performing
Stage of Team Development
Reported a Rewarding Team Experience
Brought in New $1M+ Clients
Reported No Loss of Clients

SOURCE OF INCOME
56%
19%
10%
8%
5%
2%
Salary and/or commission
Self-employed professional
Business Ownership
Retirement
Other
Inheritance

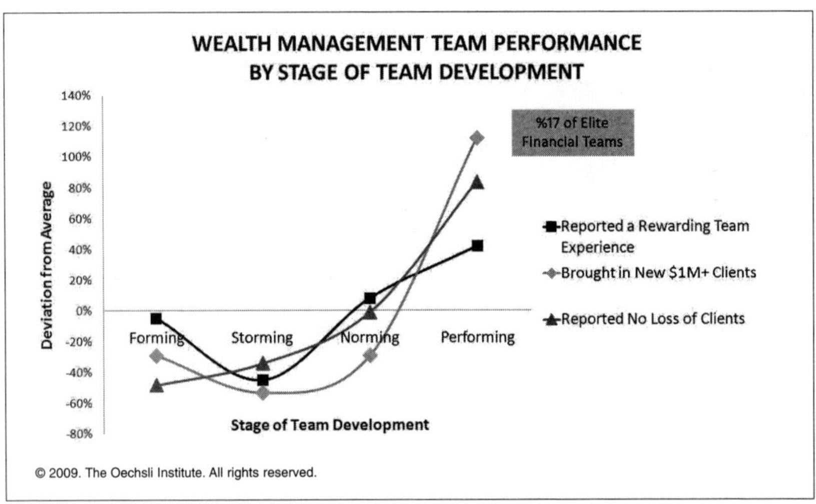

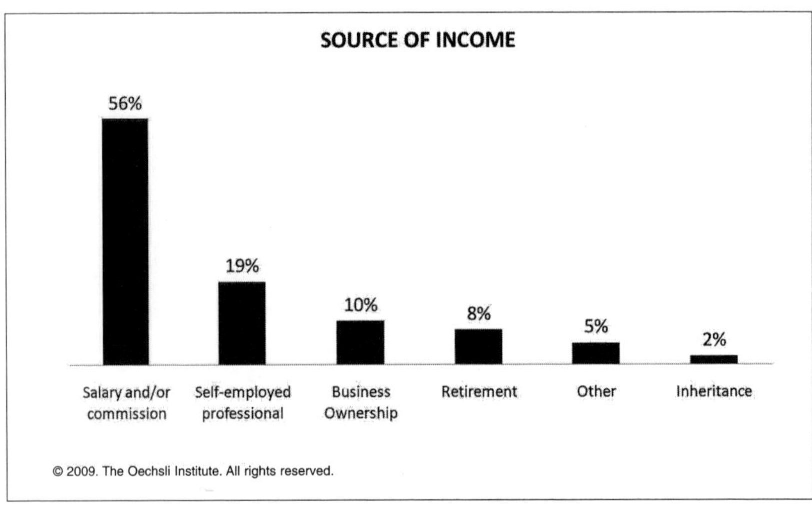

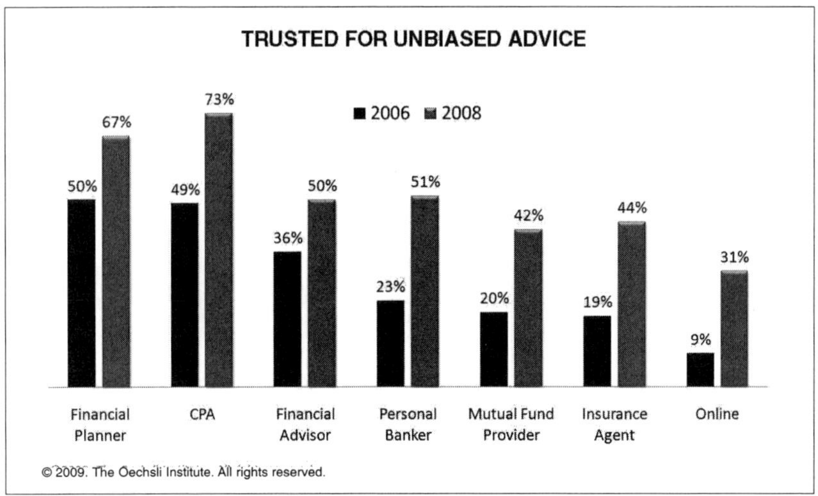
TRUSTED FOR UNBIASED ADVICE
2006
2008
50%
67%
49%
73%
36%
50%
23%
51%
20%
42%
19%
44%
9%
31%
Financial Planner
CPA
Financial Advisor
Personal Banker
Mutual Fund Provider
Insurance Agent
Online
© 2009. The Oechsli Institute. All rights reserved.

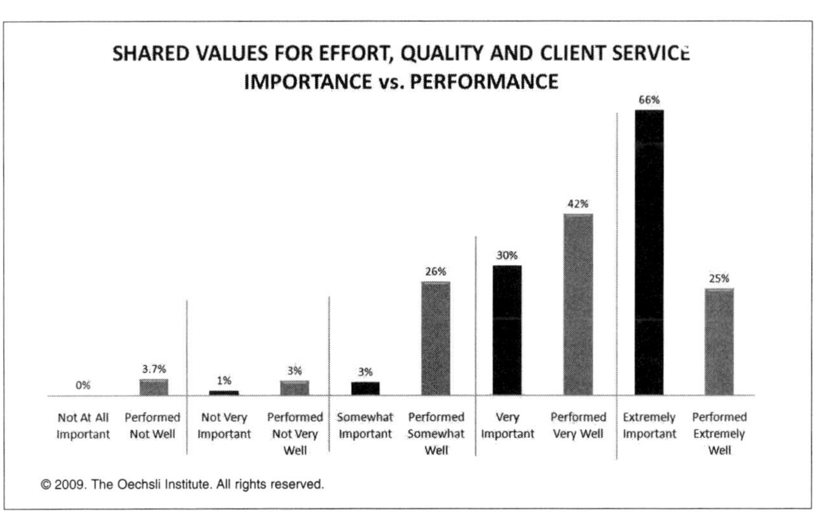
SHARED VALUES FOR EFFORT, QUALITY AND CLIENT SERVICE
IMPORTANCE vs. PERFORMANCE
0%
3.7%
1%
3%
3%
26%
30%
42%
66%
25%
Not At All Important
Performed Not Well
Not Very Important
Performed Not Very Well
Somewhat Important
Performed Somewhat Well
Very Important
Performed Very Well
Extremely Important
Performed Extremely Well
© 2009. The Oechsli Institute. All rights reserved.

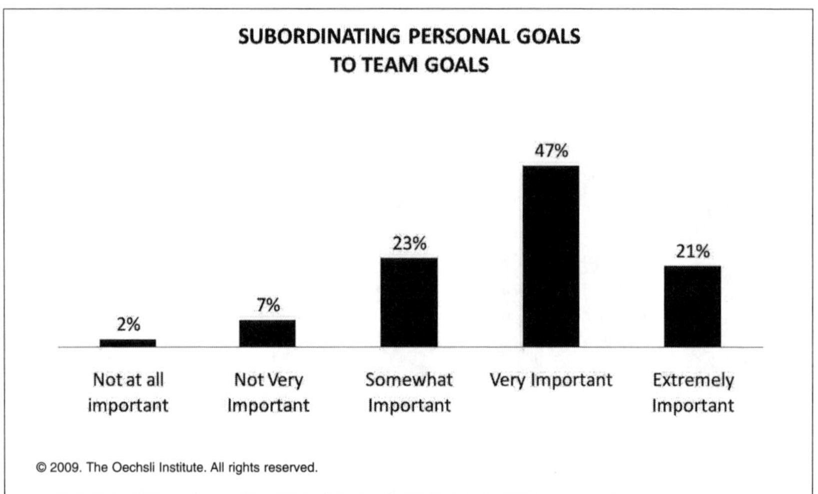
SUBORDINATING PERSONAL GOALS TO TEAM GOALS
2%
7%
23%
47%
21%
Not at all important
Not Very Important
Somewhat Important
Very Important
Extremely Important
© 2009. The Oechsli Institute. All rights reserved.

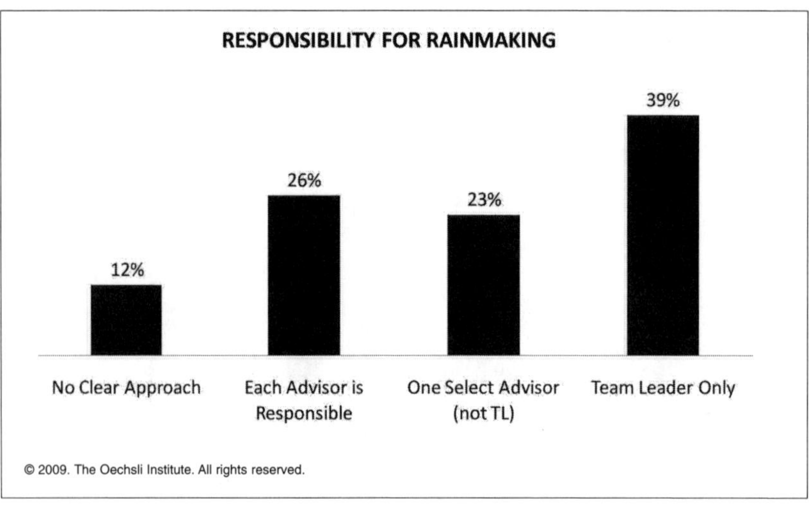
RESPONSIBILITY FOR RAINMAKING
12%
26%
23%
39%
No Clear Approach
Each Advisor is Responsible
One Select Advisor (not TL)
Team Leader Only
© 2009. The Oechsli Institute. All rights reserved.

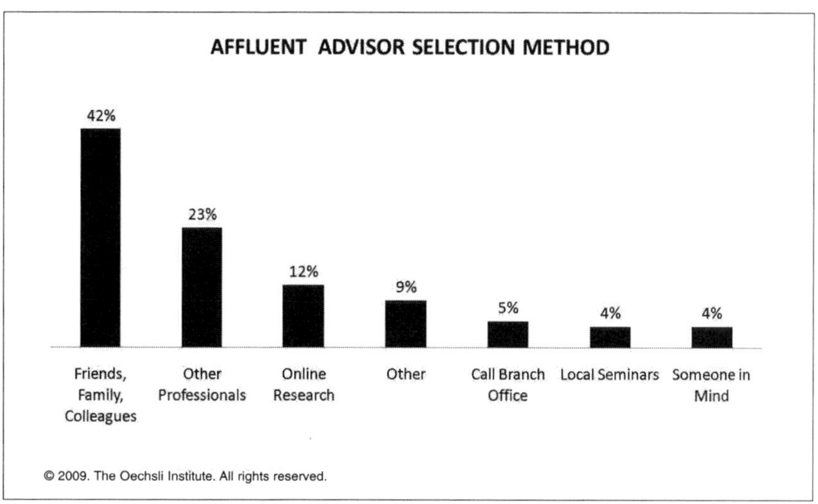
AFFLUENT ADVISOR SELECTION METHOD
42%
23%
12%
9%
5%
4%
4%
Friends, Family, Colleagues
Other Professionals
Online Research
Other
Call Branch Office
Local Seminars
Someone in Mind
© 2009. The Oechsli Institute. All rights reserved.

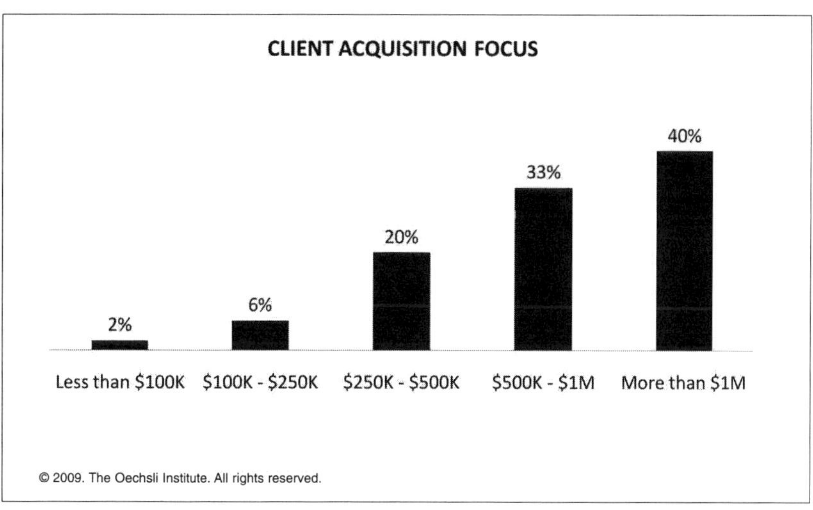
CLIENT ACQUISITION FOCUS
2%
6%
20%
33%
40%
Less than $100K
$100K - $250K
$250K - $500K
$500K - $1M
More than $1M
© 2009. The Oechsli Institute. All rights reserved.

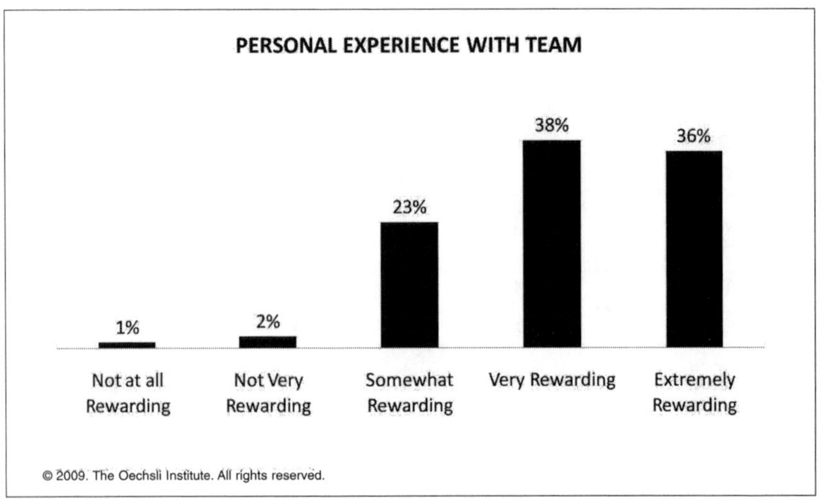
PERSONAL EXPERIENCE WITH TEAM
1%
2%
23%
38%
36%
Not at all Rewarding
Not Very Rewarding
Somewhat Rewarding
Very Rewarding
Extremely Rewarding
© 2009. The Oechsli Institute. All rights reserved.

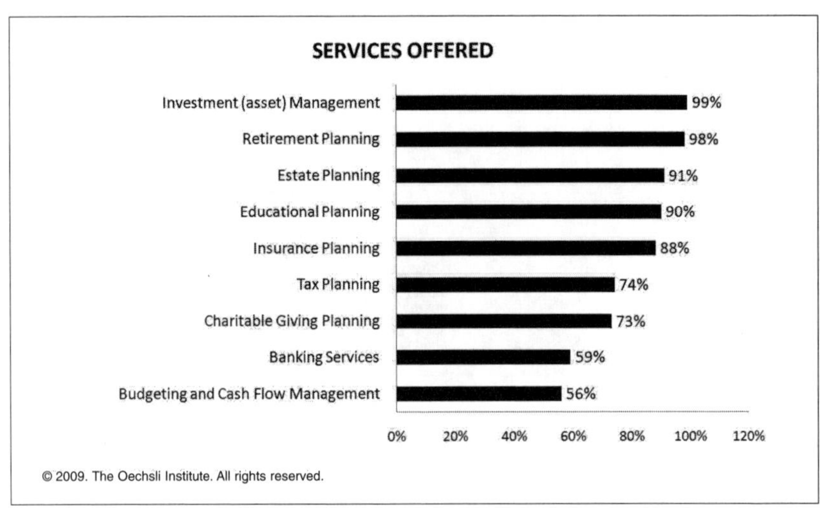
SERVICES OFFERED
Investment (asset) Management 99%
Retirement Planning 98%
Estate Planning 91%
Educational Planning 90%
Insurance Planning 88%
Tax Planning 74%
Charitable Giving Planning 73%
Banking Services 59%
Budgeting and Cash Flow Management 56%
0% 20% 40% 60% 80% 100% 120%
© 2009. The Oechsli Institute. All rights reserved.

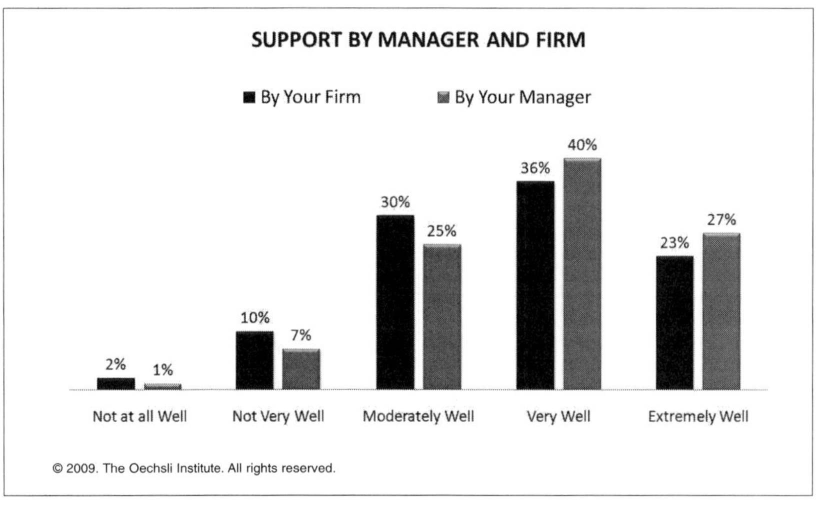
SUPPORT BY MANAGER AND FIRM
By Your Firm
By Your Manager
2%
1%
10%
7%
30%
25%
36%
40%
23%
27%
Not at all Well
Not Very Well
Moderately Well
Very Well
Extremely Well
© 2009. The Oechsli Institute. All rights reserved.

Index

About The Oechsli Institute

The Oechsli Institute, founded in 1978, is one of the leading authorities regarding marketing, selling, servicing and earning loyalty with affluent clients. They have conducted numerous research projects on the affluent. From this research, The Oechsli Institute has developed a number of training options:

Keynotes and Workshops
The Oechsli Institute conducts countless speaking engagements every year – all customized and tailored to your organization and time frame. All the information presented is research based, action oriented, and street tested.

Rainmaker Weekends
Rainmaker Weekends are 2-day action packed workshops for sales professionals who are serious about acquiring affluent clients. Learn how to better attract, service, and retain affluent clients—all based on 7 years of comprehensive research. These Weekends involve role-playing, specific do's and don'ts, all of which are important for affluent sales success.

Customized Research Projects
The Oechsli Institute conducts ongoing research projects on Elite Financial Teams, Rainmakers and the affluent.

High Performance Teams
The Oechsli Institute has conducted a comprehensive four year research project that explored the performance factors of approximately 1,000 teams. They have since developed numerous programs designed to help teams progress through the predictable stages of team development to higher levels of performance.

Performance Coaching
The Oechsli Institute works with individuals and teams who want to improve their ability to attract, service, and develop loyal affluent clients. Their clients work in collaborative relationships with a certified coach, are committed to action, and eager to experience serious growth.

Books, CDs, and DVDs
The Oechsli Institute has dozens of books, CDs, DVDs, and packages designed to improve your ability to sell to the affluent. *The Art of Selling to the Affluent* is an industry best-seller.

For more information, contact The Oechsli Institute:

The Oechsli Institute
www.Oechsli.com
info@oechsli.com
(800) 883-6582